WITNESS TO THE SPIRIT

PROCEEDINGS OF THE IRISH BIBLICAL ASSOCIATION No. 3

WITNESS TO THE SPIRIT

ESSAYS ON REVELATION, SPIRIT, REDEMPTION

Edited by

WILFRID HARRINGTON

IRISH BIBLICAL ASSOCIATION
DUBLIN
KOINONIA PRESS
MANCHESTER

Irish Biblical Association, Dublin

Koinonia Press, 19 Langdale Drive, Bury, Greater Manchester

ISBN 0 86088 017 6

*Papers read at the meetings of the Irish Biblical Association,
1975, 1976 and 1977*

CONTENTS

INTRODUCTION

It has been the policy of the Irish Biblical Association to fix a unifying theme for the papers read at its Annual General Meeting. This issue of the Proceedings of the Association presents selected papers from the meetings of 1975, 1976 and 1977 on the themes of Revelation, Spirit and Redemption. For the most part, the papers have been revised and updated for publication in 1979. It has also been our policy to round off the exegetical study of each theme with complementary contributions from systematic theologians. As it turns out, in this selection, four of the nine papers are by systematic theologians and another looks to the matter of devotion to the Holy Spirit. The volume, it is to be hoped, carries a broad appeal.

Revelation

Dr Bartlett's paper is a study of the Old Testament view of God's self-revelation in nature, work and law, and of man's response. God's revelation involves promise, and the promise shows the kind of God with whom we deal. Israel saw God as recognisably at work in creation and in the workings of nature. The hidden God reveals himself, too, through the prophets' intuitive understanding of the ways of God — an understanding that had to be proved in man's experience before it was accepted as being of abiding worth. The law came to be seen as revealing the will of Yahweh: here is where one knows the Lord. Ultimately, God was known in Israel's response to him: to know him is to obey him.

The New Testament is the concern of Dr Freyne. But he looks first to the expectation of an end-time revelation in late Judaism, expressed in wisdom and apocalyptic. Surprisingly, the personified wisdom of the Book of Wisdom and the *mysterion* of Daniel are seen to be closely related. Wisdom, the divine self-communication, is for those who are open to her invitation; in the apocalyptic setting it is only when behaviour becomes indicative of true understanding that one can speak of revelation having taken place. The ground has been laid for a consideration of the New Testament understanding of the fulness of revelation in the gospels of Mark and of John. In Mark the truth about

Jesus emerges in relation to the disciples' varied responses to his deeds and words. Throughout, the disciples are being invited to discover that the truth about Jesus can only be understood through the cross. Revelation is obviously the central theme of John. And the distinctive emphasis is that love of the brother, as Jesus loved his disciples, will bring about a true manifestation of Father and Son to the believers and a recognition that God is love. In the last analysis, revelation is God's gift of himself, freely given to his own.

Dr Ledwith rounds off the section with a consideration of modern theology of revelation. He opens with an historical perspective, noting the influence of Barth, Brunner, Tillich and Bultmann. He regrets a tendency to downgrade the rational element in faith, as well as the understanding of revelation as an attitude of faith without reference to reason's grasp on history. Then, too, some theologians have come to feel that 'revelation' can no longer be sustained as a real category in theology. Yet, the author insists, objective revelation is certainly an idea which can be retained. But how is revelation committed to man? This leads to the heart to the paper, on the mode or process of revelation, especially as it is manifested in the Bible. We are reminded of the inadequacy of our knowledge of God, even in the face of his self-revelation. And, if God has made himself known to us in extraordinary ways, we must not overlook the fact that the ordinary mode of God's communication will be through his creation in a suffused and hidden way which men of faith must discern. Revelation may be hidden and at the same time really present.

Spirit

In his study of the Holy Spirit, Dr Marsh looks first to Luke and Paul. In Luke's pneumatology, primitive and undeveloped, the Spirit is the prophetic Spirit: the power of God acting in the words and works of men with a view to the forceful presentation of God's message. It is Paul who introduced into Christian thinking the concept of the life-giving Spirit. Yet, it is only in the latter part of the second century that the pneumatology of Paul (and of John) made an impact. It took firm root in the Church's consciousness and was further developed in the fourth century. In the Western Church, however, pneumatology tended to be confined within the area of the imminant Trinity. This fact, together with the concentration of western ecclesiology on visible Church structures, meant that the theology of the Spirit — at least until our times — tended to remain abstract and remote from life.

Professor Dunn takes note of the modern Pentecostal movement and argues that we have need of a neglected gift: the discernment of spirits.

Because the Spirit of prophecy was very much a fact of their experience, the early Christians recognised the peril of false prophecy. It seems to have been Paul who grasped most clearly the danger of an inspiration whose source was demonic and whose utterance could not be trusted. Every prophetic utterance, then, must be subjected to careful scrutiny and evaluation. To this end, two criteria emerge: the character and conduct of the prophet, and the norm of earlier revelation. The responsibility of exercising discernment lies with the whole community, and the exercise of the gift involves a dialectical process. In the first place, a dialectic between the liberty of the community and the liberty of the individual. Then there are the claims of the old revelation over against the claims of the new, with a decision for the here and now. Finally, those responsible for evaluating a charism need to be open to pointers towards right assessment. Only if the crucial importance of discernment of spirits be acknowledged both by the charismatic movement and by the wider Church can that movement be held within the Church.

On a different note, Fr Corcoran reflects on aspects of the relation between doctrine and devotion. We should not reject terms like 'person' because they are open to misunderstanding: the Holy Spirit is a Person. However, we must avoid anything approaching a monism of the Spirit. The Holy Spirit is given to us in an incarnational way — given its fulness in and through the Incarnation. That is why devotion to the Holy Spirit must be adequately 'earthed'. Because, for many today, the Holy Spirit is a new discovery, there is need of appropriate catechesis. Theology of the Spirit offers few concessions to the senses, and this makes specific devotions less easy to devise. Yet, devotion to the Holy Spirit is not an optional extra for the Christian.

Redemption

While the world's redemption remains Yahweh's ultimate aim, it will come to pass only through the universal acknowledgement of Yahweh's *torah* and *mishpat*. This, argues Dr Phillips, is the view of Deuteronomy and Second Isaiah. *Torah* is a comprehensive term expressing the complete will of Yahweh, while *mishpat* is the application of Yahweh's will to the whole stratum of life. Though Israel does not envisage an active missionary role to the other nations, it must be prepared to play its role of priest nation to the world. It is as mediator of *torah* and *mishpat* that Israel is a light to the nations.

In the first of his two papers, Dr Daly looks to the theology of redemption in the Fathers. He notes that Irenaeus' doctrine of recapitulation set a pattern which Alexandrian soteriology consistently followed: the Incarnation is itself redemptive. Also, for Irenaeus, sin was a malady from which man needs to be healed. He was followed in this view by Eastern theology. The Western theology of sin borrows its characteristic models from the world of crime. This is a legacy of the North Africans who bequeathed to the West an image of God as a stern lawgiver and severe judge. Anselm of Canterbury provided the matching soteriology. The damage done to God's honour by sin could be remedied only by a great satisfaction — made by the free offering of the God-man.

In his second paper the author turns to the contemporary scene. We should recall that theories of redemption necessarily reflect our idea of God, our idea of the Church and our idea of sin. We fail to realise how difficult it is for us to accept the idea of a truly forgiving God. Nor do we really appreciate that healing and reconciliation are sacramentalised by the community's willingness to receive, to understand, to forgive and to encourage. Though we speak of the mystery of sin we end up by treating it as ethical failure. And a sociological explanation of evil is hopelessly unsatisfactory. While soteriology is not the only area of theology in trouble today, its problems are due to the fact that many of the ingredients of the traditional understanding of redemption are no longer either credible or tolerable. Any worthwhile theology of redemption has to come to terms with the cross. Finally, if we are to find models that, for our age, express the mystery of sin and redemption, we might profitably settle for alienation and reconciliation.

Revelation, Spirit, Redemption — these are certainly areas of basic Christian concern. One feels that the contributors to this volume have done not a little to light them.

Wilfrid Harrrington, O.P.

Revelation

REVELATION AND THE OLD TESTAMENT

John R. Bartlett

'The Book of Life begins with a man and woman in a garden,' said Lord Illingworth. 'It ends with Revelations,' replied Mrs Allonby. A pun is possible only when the word has more than one meaning, and the ideas in the word 'revelation', like the Revelation suitcase itself, need a good deal of unpacking. Most people do not bother, and take it that revelation refers to something about God which we cannot work out for ourselves, and our knowledge of which depends upon God's own disclosure.[1] Theologians sometimes talk about revelation as 'the self-disclosure of God'. If that is right, then in what sense or to what extent is the Old Testament 'the self-disclosure of God'? That question leads to others: how do you define the Old Testament? What do you include or exclude? How is the Old Testament related to the New Testament and 'the self-disclosure of God' you find in that? How is the Old Testament 'inspired'? What part, to put it crudely, did God play in the production of the Old Testament, and what part did man play? Where does God's self-disclosure end, and man's perception, understanding, and interpretation begin? Some of these problems will doubtless be raised in the last lecture of this conference, if not before, but for the moment my task is to raise the prior question: what did the theologians of ancient Israel who wrote the Old Testament think about God and his self-disclosure? Do the Old Testament writers speak of God as 'revealing himself', and if so, what did they mean by it?[2]

God 'reveals himself'

The phrase 'God/Yahweh revealed himself' (niphal of *galah* occurs four times in the Old Testament. According to Gen 35:7, Jacob 'built an altar, and called the place El-bethel, because there God had revealed himself to him when he fled from his brother. . .' The reference is to Jacob's dream of the ladder, the angels, and the Lord standing above the ladder (Gen 28:10ff). The point of this dream lies in the message from the Lord (Gen 28:13-15):

11

I am the Lord, the God of Abraham your father and the God of
Isaac; the land on which you lie I will give to you and to your
descendants; and your descendants shall be like the dust of the
earth, and you shall spread abroad to the west and to the east and
to the north and to the south; and by you and all your descendants shall all the families of the earth bless themselves. Behold I
am with you and will keep you wherever you go, and will bring
you back to this land; for I will not leave you until I have done
that of which I have spoken to you.

According to 1 Sam 2:27,

There came a man of God to Eli, and said to him, 'Thus the Lord
has said, "I revealed myself to the house of your father when
they were in Egypt. . . And I chose him out of all the tribes of
Israel to be my priest. . . "'

Here we are told nothing of the manner of the revelation; again, the
point lies in the message that accompanies it. In 1 Sam 3 comes the
famous story of the call of Samuel; verse seven says that Samuel did
not yet know the Lord, for the word of the Lord had not yet been
revealed to him; verse fifteen says Samuel was afraid to tell the 'vision'
to Eli. The chapter ends with the words: 'And the Lord appeared again
at Shiloh, for the Lord revealed himself to Samuel at Shiloh by the
word of the Lord' (v. 21). Revelation comes by the *word* of the Lord;
'appeared' and 'revealed himself' are very close in meaning if not
actually synonymous; the first appearance was in a 'vision' (v. 15)
whose main content was the message from the Lord of the impending
punishment of Eli's family. The Lord's self-revelation is again expressed
as a message in Isaiah 22:14 — 'The Lord of hosts has revealed himself
in my ears: "Surely this iniquity will not be forgiven you till you die,"
says the Lord God of hosts.' In short, in the four places where God is
said to have revealed himself, only one passage describes what was seen
(in a dream), and all four emphasise the message imparted—promises to
the house of Abraham and the house of Eli, and judgment on the house
of Eli and the people of Israel.

Much the same result emerges if we examine the use of the phrase
'The Lord appeared' (cf. 1 Sam 3:21 above). In Genesis the Lord
appeared to Abraham (Gen 12:7; 17:1; 18:1; cf. Exod 6:3), to Isaac
(Gen 26:24), to Jacob (Gen 35:1, 9; 48:3). In Exod 3:2, the angel of
the Lord appeared to Moses, who hid his face, 'for he was afraid to look
at God' (v. 6). In Jud 13:3ff. the angel of the Lord appeared to
Manoah's wife to announce Samson's birth; 'we shall surely die,' said
Manoah, 'for we have seen God'. The Lord appeared to Solomon in a

dream (1 Kings 3:5, cf. 2 Chron 1:7) and also a second time (1 Kings 9:2; 11:9, cf. 2 Chron 7:12). In Jer 31:3, Yahweh appears to his people, apparently in the wilderness. On all these occasions, what mattered was the message. The phrase 'The Lord' (or 'the angel of the Lord') 'appeared' is simply a way of bridging the gap between heaven and earth and gives no clue to the nature of the Lord (except that he can bridge that gap). What is revealed on each occasion is a promise — for the future of the people, the birth of a child, the gift of wisdom, the establishment of a dynasty, the restoration of Israel. The promises show with what kind of God we are dealing; but God himself in his essential being remains hidden, as the Old Testament authors understood: the sight of God carries the risk of death.

Seeing God

A number of people are said to have seen God, and lived. What did they see, and how much of God did it reveal? Gen 28:13 describes Jacob's ladder, 'and behold the Lord God stood above it'; presumably the author thinks this is what Jacob saw. In Gen 32:30, Jacob names the place Peniel, 'for I have seen God face to face, and yet my life is preserved'. According to Exod 24:9-11,

> Then Moses and Aaron, Nadab and Abihu, and seventy of the elders of Israel went up, and they saw the God of Israel; and there was under his feet as it were a pavement of sapphire stone, like the very heaven for clearness. And he did not lay his hand on the chief men of the people of Israel; they beheld God, and ate and drank.[3]

The only description is of what is under God's feet; and it is noted that those who saw God remain unscathed: 'he did not lay his hand' on them. In Exod 33:18ff. Moses is given only a limited view of God: God warns him that 'you cannot see my face; for man shall not see me and live', and says 'you shall see my back; but my face shall not be seen'. Compare, too, Manoah's remark in Jud 13:22. But the Psalmist can cry,

> So I have looked upon thee in the sanctuary,
>   beholding thy power and glory (Ps 63:2),

and we are reminded of Isaiah's temple vision:

> I saw the Lord sitting upon a throne, high and lifted up; and his train filled the temple. Above him stood the seraphim; each had six wings; with two he covered his face, and with two he covered his feet, and with two he flew. And one called to another and said:

13

'Holy, holy, holy is the Lord of hosts,
the whole earth is full of his glory'.

The prophet Micaiah ben Imlah sees something very similar (1 Kings 22:19):

> I saw the Lord sitting on his throne, and all the host of heaven standing beside him on his right hand and on his left; and the Lord said, 'Who will entice Ahab...?'

Similarly, in Is 40:1-11, the prophet hears voices at the heavenly court, telling him the message he is to preach. The prophet says nothing of seeing anything; what matters (as in the case of Micaiah ben Imlah and Isaiah) is the message given to him. The most explicit prophetic vision of God is perhaps Ezekiel's, though Ezekiel is careful to speak only of 'a likeness as it were of human form' whose upper half is as bright as gleaming bronze and whose lower half bright as fire — 'the appearance of the likeness of the glory of the Lord' (1:28). The vision here , too, is the preface to a message.

Sometimes one sees not the Lord, directly, but his glory.[4] What does this reveal of Yahweh? The glory appears 'like a devouring fire' on top of Sinai (Exod 24:17). The peoples behold the glory of Yahweh who manifests himself with clouds, darkness, fire, lightnings, and mountains melting like wax (Ps 97:1-6). According to Exod 40:34f., the cloud covered the tent of meeting and the glory of the Lord filled the tabernacle; according to 1 Kings 8:11, 'the glory of the Lord filled the house of the Lord', together with a cloud, at the dedication of Solomon's temple. The psalmist saw God's power and glory in the sanctuary (Ps 63:2). The glory seems originally to have belonged to theophanies of Yahweh and to have become particularly associated with the presence of Yahweh in the tabernacle, tent, or temple, where the worshipper may claim to see it. It is associated with God's attributes of strength (Ps 29:1, 4; Ps 63:2) and royalty (Ps 29:1, 10f.; Ps 97:1, 6; Is 6:1-5), but also with God's goodness, grace and mercy (Exod 33:18-23). Moses asks to see God's glory, and is answered,

> I will make all my goodness pass before you, and will proclaim before you my name 'The Lord'; and I will be gracious to whom I will be gracious, and will show mercy on whom I will show mercy.[5]

In one strand of the Priestly writing, the glory appears in order 'to establish and legitimate the cult'[6] (cf. Exod 24:15ff., 40:34f., Lev 9: 6, 23). Similarly Ezekiel connects the glory of the Lord with the presence of Yahweh in the temple and its worship. And the association of the glory with the theophany of Yahweh and his power is extended into the future: Deutero-Isaiah has the eschatological hope and conviction that 'the glory of the Lord shall be revealed / and all flesh shall see it together,' which he couples with the message, 'Behold, the Lord God comes with might, / and his arm rules for him' (Is 40:5, 10).

As one reflects upon this material, much of which has clear links with the cult and cultic places, it becomes clear that seeing the Lord and his glory did not in itself provide much by way of immediate or direct revelation of God's self or being. The same is true of the expression 'to behold the face' of God.[7] Jacob saw God face to face at Peniel, Moses spoke with the Lord face to face in the tent (Exod 33:11), the psalmist prayed (Ps 42:2): 'My soul thirsts for God, for the living God. / When shall I come and behold the face of God?' Another psalmist asks, 'how long wilt thou hide thy face from me?' (Ps 13:1), and another knows that the eyes of the Lord might be towards the righteous and the face of the Lord against evildoers (34:16). It is not always clear how literally these expressions were meant: in Ps 17:15, the worshipper ends his prayer with the words, 'As for me, I shall behold thy face in righteousness; / when I awake, I shall be satisfied with beholding thy form,' which according to Weiser[8] allude to a theophany expected to take place in the cult the following morning (cf. v. 3), and according to Snaith[9] have 'a more spiritual reference to the inward reality of communion which lies behind'. But basically, 'beholding the face' probably 'meant to be admitted to the presence of the potentate, king or god' — i.e. gaining an audience. Compare 1 Kings 13:6, where Jeroboam says to the man of God, 'Entreat now the favour' (literally, 'entreat now the face') 'of the Lord your God, and pray for me'. A man went to the sanctuary to gain an audience with God and get an answer to his prayer. In Ps 80, the psalmist prays to God, enthroned upon the cherubim, 'Restore us, O God; / let thy face shine, that we may be saved!' If God is to be revealed to the worshipper, it is through his promise to the worshipper, the presence, the comfort, the help, the forgiveness, the salvation that he brings in response to the worshipper's petition, the mighty acts he performs on behalf of Israel or the distressed Israelite. God may be revealed, in so far as 'revealed' is the right word, in his word through the prophet, his command through the law and the priest, his wisdom through the wise man, his presence in events, and in natural phenomena. It is here, in particular, that we meet the theophany. Yahweh's power to act for Israel or an Israelite is often described in terms of Yahweh's theophany, his appearance or presence in natural phenomena.[10] Thus when the author of Ps 18 in his distress calls on God for help,

From his temple he heard my voice,
    and my cry to him reached his ears.
Then the earth reeled and rocked;
    the foundations also of the mountains trembled
    and quaked, because he was angry.
smoke went up from his nostrils,
    and devouring fire from his mouth;
    glowing coals flamed forth from him.
He bowed the heavens and came down;
    thick darkness was under his feet.
He rode upon a cherub and flew,
    he came swiftly upon the wings of the wind.
He made darkness his covering round about him,
    his canopy thick clouds dark with water.
Out of the brightness before him
    there broke through his clouds
    hailstones and coals of fire.
The Lord also thundered in the heavens,
    and the Most High unttered his voice,
    hailstones and coals of fire.
And he sent out his arrows and scattered them;
    he flashed forth his lightnings and routed them.
Then the channels of the sea were seen,
    and the foundations of the earth were laid bare,
at thy rebuke, O Lord,
    at the blast of the breath of thy nostrils.

He reached from on high, he took me,
    he drew me out of many waters,
He delivered me from my strong enemy. . . (Ps 18:6-16)

We should compare similar manifestations described in Ps 29, Ps 50:3, Ps 77:11-29, Amos 1:2. Best known in this context is Jud 5:4f:

Lord, when thou didst go forth from Seir,
    when thou didst march from the region of Edom,
the earth trembled,
    and the heavens dropped,
    yea, the clouds dropped water.
The mountains quaked before the Lord,
    yon Sinai before the Lord, the God of Israel.

These poetic, hymnic passages, probably used in Israel's worship or on formal public occasions of rejoicing, recount Yahweh's presence with and for his people (or an individual) with the help of vivid descriptions of the accompanying physical and natural phenomena. In so describing the power and presence of Yahweh, the ancient Israelite was following an older tradition: thus, for example, the Canaanite described his god Baal-hadad with the epithet *rkb 'rpt*, 'He who mounteth the clouds', an epithet adopted for Yahweh in Deut 33:26 (cf. Ps 18:11, Ps 68:4, Is 19:1).[11] This traditional description of the divine power, borrowed from religions which focussed on the power in nature, is used by the Israelite cultic tradition to heighten the reference to Yahweh's activity on behalf of Israel on certain major occasions. It is hardly surprising to find the Sinai event presented in terms of storm or volcanic phenomena (E and J respectively, according to Clements[12]), or the Exodus event presented alongside older myths of creation (cf. Is 51:9f). Theophanies *via* natural phenomena were not new in the world of ancient Israel, but the events of Sinai and Exodus were the experience of Israel, or seminal groups which founded Israel, alone. The experiences of Sinai and Exodus are basic to Israel's understanding of her religion, and here if anywhere we might expect to find any 'revelation' that was given to Israel. But even here the Old Testament tradition does not emphasise the idea that in these events God 'revealed himself' (though it does appear: cf. Deut 4:32ff., or Ezek 20: 'On the day when I chose Israel... making myself known to them in the land of Egypt, I swore to them, saying, I am the Lord your God'.) The Old Testament emphasis is rather that here God redeemed Israel, gave them a law, and demanded obedience. The emphasis is on the message rather than the theophany. The point can be seen clearly in 1 Kings 19:9-13, where Elijah is told to stand on the mount before the Lord.

> And behold, the Lord passed by, and a great and strong wind rent the mountains and broke in pieces the rocks before the Lord, but the Lord was not in the wind; and after the wind an earthquake, but the Lord was not in the earthquake; and after the earthquake a fire, but the Lord was not in the fire; and after the fire a still small voice.

None of these mighty theophanic acts in fact reveals Yahweh. They were the preface to the voice which gave Elijah his commission. And elsewhere in the Old Testament tradition, the revelation lies not in the theophanies, but in the experience whose importance for Israel is underlined by the theophanies. The theophany is the sign accompanying the real message.

God revealed in Nature

It is clear, of course, from the theophany tradition, that Isarel, like her neighbours, saw God as recognisably at work in creation and in the workings of nature. Naturally, for God was creator: 'The heavens are telling the glory of God / and the firmament proclaims his handiwork.' The most urgent seeker after God in the Old Testament is Job: 'Oh, that I knew where I might find him, that I might come even to his seat!' (23:3), and the Lord answers him 'out of the whirlwind' (38:1; 40:6), challenging him with a series of questions which emphasise God's power in creation — 'Where were you when I laid the foundation of the earth? Tell me, if you have understanding' (38:4) — until Job submits:

> I had heard of thee by the hearing of the ear,
>   but now my eye sees thee;
> therefore I despise myself,
>   and repent in dust and ashes (42:5).

'No physical vision is implied,' says Rowley, 'but an experience of God that was real and personal. The hope of 19:27 has been realised, but not after death.'[13] What was revealed, and what was experienced, was man's situation before God; the medium of revelation was the world of nature and creation. There are many other places which reflect the Israelite belief that God was at work in creation; but other nations believed this too, and Jeremiah warns Israel that it is possible to misread the evidence of heaven:

> Learn not the way of the nations,
>   nor be dismayed at the signs of the heavens
>   because the nations are dismayed at them,
> for the customs of the peoples are false (Jer 10:2f).

The astrology-minded Babylonians understood 'meteors, comets and other celestial phenomena as portents of events to be brought about by the gods on earth'.[14] How does one know (one might ask) what is revelatory, and what is not? Or if all is in a sense revelatory, by what criteria can one interpret it? And (one might add) if its interpretation is doubtful, in what sense is anything revealed?

God revealed in the Prophetic Word

Certainty of receiving a communication from Yahweh is one of the most important and most appealing things about the prophets of Israel. The prophets are conscious of being called to their task, of being under some compulsion, of carrying the Lord's message from the heavenly council which they have attended. Their cry is 'Thus saith the Lord', and they speak, interestingly, of both hearing and seeing the word of the Lord. The book of Amos begins, 'The words of Amos . . . which he saw concerning Israel', and Amos uses the phrase, 'Thus the Lord God showed me' (7:1, 4, cf. 7:7; 8:1) and he sees the Lord forming locusts, calling for judgment by fire, holding a plumb line, and standing by the altar (9:1). In one case the Lord simply shows Amos a basket of summer fruit. Micaiah ben Imlah saw Israel scattered on the mountains, as sheep without a shepherd; Jeremiah saw a rod of almond. In each case, the natural object or event seen is the medium of revelation and conveys to the prophet a message of the Lord's activity. The almond rod and the basket of summer fruit are particularly interesting, for the message comes by way of association of words; Jeremiah sees an almond rod (*shaqed*) and interprets this to mean that the Lord is watching (*shoqed*) over his word to perform it. Revelation has come to others in similar manner; Brockington[15] quotes Augustine's experience: 'I heard a voice from some neighbour's house, as it had been of a boy or of a girl, I know not whether, in a singing tune saying, and often repeating, Take up and read. . . ' In this sort of vision, the prophet's experience of the Lord starts with his experience of something quite mundane. If he says that he sees the Lord, what he describes is a common object; and the important thing is not what is seen but its meaning, which is usually judgment. The Lord reveals, through the prophet's intuitive understanding of some object, what he is going to do to Israel. The Lord himself remains hidden, but 'does nothing without revealing his secret to his servants the prophets'. That revelation came through the prophet's physical life and environment. 'His experience of God and his work for God were not things outside ordinary life, they were life itself, and every part of life and every event and natural object was potentially an instrument for God's use.[16] Thus Hosea learned God's message through his marital experience, and Ezekiel, as a priest, through what happened to the temple. For Isaiah, he and his children were 'signs and portents in Israel', contrasted, apparently, as a source of knowledge with mediums and wizards who chirp and mutter (Is 8:18f). But if the revelation comes through, and is expressed in terms of, what are otherwise normal experiences of life, it is not always easy for the prophet's audience to distinguish between what is genuine and what is not. Jeremiah complains of prophets who 'speak visions of their own minds, not from the mouth of the Lord' (Jer 23:16), who 'prophesy lying dreams':

> I did not send the prophets, yet they ran;
> I did not speak to them, yet they prophesied.
> But if they had stood in my council,
> then they would have proclaimed my words to my people.

Jeremiah says of himself that

> Then the Lord put forth his hand and touched my mouth;
> and the Lord said to me,
>> Behold, I have put my words in your mouth. (Jer 1:9).

The prophet was conscious of proclaiming something from the Lord, something not his own. 'He was the mouthpiece of God, bringing some *ad hoc* word relevant to the circumstances of the moment when he delivered it. But since the inspiration came through the organ of the prophet's personality, it bore the marks of that personality as well as of the God who was its source. Hence not all the prophets were of the same stature, and there are varieties of level even within the same prophetic books.'[17] Presumably, the more of his own personality a prophet intruded into his message, the more it revealed of him and the less it revealed of God. and then as now, the hearer had to exercise discernment. The Deuteronomist applies the acid, but slow, test: 'when a prophet speaks in the name of the Lord, if the word does not come to pass or come true, that is a word which the Lord has not spoken' (Deut 28:22). Micaiah ben Imlah made the same point to the king of Israel: 'If you return in peace, the Lord has not spoken to me' (1 Kings 22:28). And it is because Micaiah turned out to be right, presumably, that his story has been preserved. The prophetic understanding of God's purposes had to be proved in man's experience before it was accepted as being of abiding worth, and even after acceptance, its precise interpretation might be debated. If God reveals his purpose, man may still misunderstand or reject the message. Acceptance is an act of faith.

God revealed in the Law

He that says 'that the Law is not from heaven' will be among those that have no share in the world to come, according to the Mishnah (San 10. 1). Simeon the Just (cf. Ecclus 50), c. 200 BC, used to say, 'By three things is the world sustained: by the Law, by the (temple) service, and by deeds of loving kindness' (Aboth 1. 2). Judas Maccabee's father urged his sons 'to show zeal for the law' (1 Macc 2:50). The perfect scribe 'devotes himself to the study of the law of the Most High' and will 'glory in the law of the Lord's covenant' (Ecclus 39:1-8). The Psalmist cries,

> Oh, how I love thy law!
>> It is my meditation all the day...
> I have more understanding than my teachers,
>> for thy testimonies are my meditation...
> Thy word is a lamp unto my feet

and a light to my path. (Ps 119:97, 99, 105, cf. Ps 19:7ff).

Jesus ben Sirach poetically identified 'the law which Moses commanded us', which gives wisdom and understanding (24:23ff), with the personified figure of Wisdom, who says of herself, 'I came forth from the mouth of the Most High', and was then given a home in Zion (24:2, 8-12). The author of Ps 40 professes his obedience: 'I delight to do thy will, O my God; / thy law is within my heart.' Psalm 1 praises the man whose delight is in the law of the Lord and who meditates on it daily. In post-exilic Jewish piety, the law expresses God's will and brings wisdom and understanding. It has gained its honoured place, naturally, in a long history of development. The Mishnah refers to the importance of the 'men of the Great Synagogue' who came with Ezra (Aboth 1. 1); the decree of Artaxerxes calls Ezra 'the scribe of the law of the God of Heaven' and authorised him to teach the laws of his God, putting the Jewish law on a par with the Persian law: 'Whoever will not obey they law of your God and the law of the king, let judgment be strictly executed upon him' (Ezra 7:26) — a very important development indeed. Sometime before Ezra came the Priestly writer (c. 550-540 BC?), writing to prepare his people for the post-exilic reconstruction of national life. He produces a history of Israel from the beginnings in creation to Israel's arrival on the edge of the promised land, emphasising the promises of future blessing and emphasising that the link between man and God lies in the cult and the law.[18] The observance of the Sabbath (Gen 2:2f), the prohibition of eating blood or shedding man's blood (Gen 9:2-6), the command to circumcise (Gen 17:9-14), and the instructions for the cult and priesthood (Exod 25ff) are based directly on the activity or command of God. God blessed the seventh day, gave Noah the Noachian commands, gave Abraham the command to circumcise, and told Moses to make the tabernacle and its furniture 'according to all that I show you' (Exod 25:9). All the subsequent directions for sacrifice, priesthood, and so on, are given with the formula, 'The Lord said to Moses (and Aaron)'. The Priestly writer gives direct divine authority — the status of revelation, you might say — to those aspects of tradition and behaviour and cultic practice which as a result of the exile seem to him to have become vital for the ongoing life of Israel. He is also careful to stress the importance of God's name and make this also a matter of revelation.

God said to Moses, 'I am the Lord. I appeared to Abraham, to Isaac, and to Jacob, as God Almighty, but by my name the Lord I did not make myself known to them. . . Say therefore to the people of Israel, "I am the Lord and I will bring you out from

21

under the burdens of the Egyptians. . . and I will take you for my people, and I will be your God; and you shall know that I am the Lord your God, who has brought you out from under the burdens of the Eygptians. And I will bring you into the land which I swore to give to Abraham, to Isaac, and to Jacob; I will give it to you for a possession. I am the Lord.' (Exod 6:2-8)

This passage is important for our theme. It contrasts the revelation given to the patriarchs and that given to Moses. A new name is given, in the repeated formula, 'I am Yahweh', combined with the promise of deliverance from Egypt, a covenant relationship with God, and the gift of land. 'The name of Yahweh functions as a guarantee that the reality of God stands behind the promise and will execute its fulfilment.'[19] The revelation of the name guarantees also the divine commands already given and the cultic laws about to be given; they are the expression of Yahweh's will for Israel. Revelation for P was progressive and culminated in what was revealed through Moses. The Priestly work marks an important stage in Israel's understanding of what God had revealed to her.

Equally important was the part played by the Deuteronomistic tradition. This tradition had a very high respect for the Deuteronomic code: the king himself must copy it, read it and keep it (Deut 17:18ff); Moses wrote this law and commanded that it be read every seven years publicly (Deut 31:9ff). No word must be added or taken from it (4:2). There is frequent exhortation to keep the statutes and commandments; blessings and curses are provided for obedience or disobedience to 'the voice of the Lord your God' (28:1ff, 15ff). These commandments are as much the word of the Lord, it seems, as are prophetic oracles; and just as the Isaianic teaching and testimony could be bound up and sealed among the disciples, so the words of this law could be written in a book (Deut 28:58). Hilkiah found the book of the law in the temple, and Shaphan read it to the king; 'and when the king heard the words of the book of the law, he rent his clothes'. Josiah's subsequent acts show he took the book seriously; was it 'revelation' to him? He consulted a prophetess, and perhaps in the end accepted the book as authoritative because it came with the backing of both prophetic advice and its temple provenance, and because of its own intrinsic authority. Here was a collection of legal material which influenced a cultic reformation and became the basis for the religious life of the individual Israelite. It has often been suggested that the arrival of Deuteronomy marked the beginnings of 'a religion of the book'. But if such a book was coming to be seen as the basis of religion, and of knowledge of Yahweh, there was one prophet who saw further:

> Behold, the days are coming, says the Lord, when I will make a
> new covenant with the house of Israel and the house of Judah. . .
> I will put my law within them, and I will write it upon their
> hearts; and I will be their God, and they shall be my people. And
> no longer shall each man teach his neighbour and each his brother,
> saying, 'Know the Lord, for they shall all know me, from the
> least of them to the greatest, says the Lord, for I will forgive their
> iniquity, and I will remember their sin no more. (Jer 31:31-34).

'My law' must be put within human hearts; it is not enough to have a
book of it.[20] And then 'they shall all know me'.

This is not the place to trace the complex origins and development
of the laws and lawcodes of ancient Israel. But it is important for our
purpose to notice the way in which laws and groups of laws and lawcodes were from early times given authority by being connected with
the name of Yahweh. As is well known, the Decalogue is prefaced with
the formula, 'I am the Lord your God, who brought you out of the
land of Egypt, out of the house of bondage' (Exod 20:2, cf. Deut 5:6).
Rendtorff comments, 'God's law is therefore proclaimed in express
connection with the previous history of Yahweh with Israel in which
Yahweh is portrayed as the God who continually leads and protects
his people. The law obtains its authority from this self-manifestation
of God in the history of Israel'.[21] Similarly, in Lev 19, for example,
the law is presented as part of the speech of Yahweh (Lev 19:1), and
individual commands have attached to them the phrase 'I am the
Lord': e.g., 'You shall not go up and down as a slanderer among your
people, and you shall not stand forth against the life of your neighbour: I am the Lord' (19:16). The law, whatever its human origin,
comes to be seen as revealing the will of Yahweh. This is where one
knows the Lord. [22]

Knowing God

Jeremiah 31:31ff argued that under the coming new covenant the present ineffective teaching of the law would be replaced by a situation in
which, with the law written in their hearts, men would know the Lord.
As Gerald Downing pointed out, in the Old Testament 'to know God' is
virtually the equivalent of 'to obey God'.[23] Thus in 1 Sam 2:12: 'The
sons of Eli were worthless men; they had no regard for the Lord' (literally, 'they did not know the Lord'); compare the cases of others who
do not know the Lord — Pharaoh (Exod 5:2), Israel (Hos 8:1-3,
Is 1:3ff), the heathen (Ps 79:6). 'It is obvious from these people's
actions that they do not know God. They disobey him, and that is why

23

it is said that they do not "know him". The "knowing" and the "obeying" are really the same activity.' Thus in Exod 33:13, Moses prays God, 'Show me now they ways, that I may know thee and find favour in thy sight'. 1 Chron 28:8f makes David say to Solomon, 'Know the God of your father, and serve him with a whole heart and a willing mind'. In Is 19:21, the prophet says,

> And the Lord will make himself known to the Egyptians; and the Egyptians will know the Lord in that day and worship with sacrifice and burnt offerings, and they will make vows to the Lord and perform them.

Knowing the Lord will be expressed by cultic activity as demanded in the law. In a famous criticism of king Jehoiakim, Jeremiah says,

> Did not your father eat and drink and do justice and righteousness?
> Then it was well with him.
> He judged the cause of the poor and needy;
> then it was well.
> Is not this to know me?
> says the Lord. (Jer 22:15f)

Compare Hos 4:1:

> There is no faithfulness or kindness,
> and no knowledge of God in the land;[24]

and Hos 6:6:

> For I desire steadfast love and not sacrifice,
> the knowledge of God, rather than burnt offerings.

There are similar implications about the meaning of knowing God in Jer 9:24:

> Let him who glories glory in this, that he understands and knows me, that I am the Lord who practise steadfast love, justice, and righteousness in the earth; for in these things I delight, says the Lord.

Knowledge of God means knowledge of his demands, here again introduced by the formula 'I am the Lord'.

The verb 'to know' is sometimes used in the Old Testament with the formula 'I am the Lord' or something similar as its object.[25] What is it that leads to that knowledge, and what does that knowledge include? The plagues, for example, are sent to Pharaoh 'that you may know that there is no one like the Lord our God' (Exod 8:10, cf. 9:14, 29). 'Knowing' here is not very different from 'fearing', as is shown by Exod

14:31: 'And Israel saw the great work which the Lord did against the Egyptians, and the people feared the Lord'. Jethro (Exod 18:11) says, 'Now I know that the Lord is greater than all gods, because he delivered the people from under the hand of the Egyptians'.[26] After being cleansed of his leprosy, Naaman said, 'Behold, I know that there is no God in all the earth but in Israel' (2 Kings 5:15). There is certainly a tradition in Israel that 'revelation' came through what God did for Israel, and it is well summed up in a passage from the introduction to Deuteronomy (4:32ff):

> For ask now of the days that are past, which were before you, since the day that God created man upon the earth, and ask from one end of heaven to the other, whether such a great thing as this has ever happened or was ever heard of. Did any people ever hear the voice of a god speaking out of the midst of the fire, as you have heard, and still live? Or has any god ever attempted to go and take a nation for himself from the midst of another nation, by trials, by signs, by wonders, and by war, by a mighty hand and an outstretched arm, and by great terrors, according to all that the Lord your God did for you in Egypt before your eyes? To you it was shown, that you might know that the Lord is God; there is no other besides him. Out of heaven he let you hear his voice, that he might discipline you; and on earth he let you see his great fire, and you heard his words out of the midst of the fire... Therefore you shall keep his statutes and commandments...

'Revelation' came through the events of Exodus and Sinai, 'that you might know that the Lord is God', which is as much as to say, 'that he might discipline you'. Knowledge of God means, as before, obedience. And that knowledge came from Israel's experience, from signs and wonders, from seeing the fire and hearing the voice. But knowledge of Yahweh might come from future experience, as well as past experience. Thus in the ninth century BC.,

> a prophet came near to Ahab king of Israel, and said, 'Thus says the Lord, Have you seen all this great multitude? Behold, I will give it into you hand this day; and you shall know that I am the Lord' (1 Kings 20:13. cf. v. 28).

In Is 45:3, the Lord says to Cyrus,

> I will give you the treasures of darkness
>   and the hoards in secret places,
> that you may know that it is I, the Lord,
>   the God of Israel, who call you by your name...

25

Ezekiel uses this language frequently: e.g., Ezek 36:23,

> And I will vindicate the holiness of my great name, which has been profaned among the nations, and which you have profaned among them; and the nations will know that I am the Lord, says the Lord God, when through you I vindicate my holiness before their eyes.

Compare Ps 98:2:

> The Lord has made known his victory,
>   he has revealed his vindication in the sight of the nations.
> He has remembered his steadfast love and faithfulness
>   to the house of Israel.
> All the ends of the earth have seen the victory of our God.[28]

What is revealed, or to be revealed, is God's vindication of Israel and thereby of his own holiness. The vindication is yet to come for Ezekiel, or has come in some event hymned by the psalmist. There is in ancient Israel as in Christian theology a double-endedness about revelation: it has roots in the past and consummation in the future, and we live between the two of them in in their light.

This is borne out when we consider, finally, those few passages in the Old Testament where it is said that Yahweh made himself or will make himself known (niphal of *yadah*). Exod 6:3 and Is 19:21 have already been mentioned: Exod 6:3 refers to the new statement of divine promises and their fulfilment to Moses, and the second is dated 'in that day' and refers to the future day of the Lord. The psalmist uses the word to refer to Israel's experience of Jerusalem as God's dwelling place: 'Within her citadels God / has shown himself a sure defence (Ps 48:3). According to Ezek 20:5, 9 God made himself known to Israel in bringing them out of the land of Egypt; according to Ezek 35: 11, 38:23, God will make himself known to Edom and other nations in acts of judgment. God is known in past experience and will be known, it is hoped, in future vindication of Israel or punishment of her enemies. It is then, as Deutero-Isaiah puts it, that 'the glory of the Lord shall be revealed, and all flesh shall see it together' (40:5). That should lead to a consideration of what ancient Israel expected to see of the Lord 'on that day', but this is not the place to catalogue the many varieties of Israel's eschatological hopes. It is time to draw some conclusions.

Revelation and Response

If the ancient Israelites thought of God as 'revealing himself' to them, it was in an indirect and limited way. God is known through appearances to the founding fathers and other special people, through seeing him or his glory or his face in the cult, through observing his power in nature, through hearing his word in the prophetic oracles and meeting his demands in the law, and through experiencing his help in the course of history.[29] But it is nowhere suggested that God's whole self or essential being is revealed; rather, revelation takes a variety of forms, in none of which is God revealed in any full sense. God's purpose, power, will and other attributes may be known, to some extent, through events, situations, persons — through very earthen vessels, in fact. God might make a prophet the bearer of his word, but the word is received and expressed through very human means. 'If there is a prophet among you, I the Lord make myself known to him in a vision, I speak with him in a dream. Not so with my servant Moses... with him I speak mouth to mouth, clearly, and not in dark speech; and he beholds the form of the Lord' (Num 12:6-8). Moses, indeed, is exceptional, the prophet *par excellence*: but what is revealed through him is the divine demand which nevertheless had a very long and complicated human history both before and after becoming recognised as a divine demand. The power of God might be seen in the events of the past, present, and future, and recounted as history — events as various as the flood, the exodus, the fall of Jerusalem, and the day of the Lord — but different historians might select different events and understand them in different ways — P and J, Kings and Chronicles show their different approaches.

In ancient Israel, as elsewhere, it was generally speaking only with benefit of hindsight that laws, prophetic oracles, interpretations of history, understanding of the world, became accepted as 'divinely authorised' or 'revealed'. It took time for collections of history, prophecy, wisdom, law, and liturgical material to grow and become accepted as the prime source for the understanding of God's relationship with Israel. And yet from the early days of Yahwism the demand of Yahweh was there, recognised and interpreted by way of law and prophetic oracle and history and wise saying and liturgy. God was known in Israel's response to him; to know him is to obey him. The response is in a sense the revealing thing; but as no Israelite responded perfectly, so revelation is not perfect. The Israelites knew as well as the Christian knew that works are a response to grace. But where does grace stop and where do works begin? Where does 'revelation' stop and man's recognition of it begin?[30] Israelite and Christian alike know that they cannot be separated, at least not in this world, for all is not yet revealed and all is not yet recognised. It was a Hebrew of the Hebrews and yet an apostle of Jesus who said that 'now we see in a mirror darkly, but then face to face. Now I know in part; then I shall understand fully, even as

27

Israelite' (p. 115). Jer 31:31-34 'refers to knowledge of the Torah as read in the Synagogue service' (p. 114). As the prophet appears to rule out the need for future teaching, I am not convinced by Swetnam's suggestion; but in any case, knowledge of Yahweh remains for the prophet an unfulfilled hope for the future.

21. Rendtorff, op. cit., p. 41.

22. Cf. Rendtorff, ibid,, 'The name YHWH must be here presupposed as known and carrying such weight that commands emanating from this God have an authority that is unambiguously binding.'

23. F. G. Downing, *Has Christianity a Revelation?*, London (1964), pp. 37-45. See also on *yada'* J. Weingreen, 'Some Observations on English Versions of the Old Testament', in *Hermathena* (1972), pp. 5-14: see section V, p. 11f.

24. Weingreen, ibid, p. 12: 'The literal translation adopted by all the English versions, "there is no knowledge of God in the land", suggests mass ignorance about God, whereas what the prophet is denouncing is the total abandonment of all religious and moral principles.'

25. See Rendtorff, op. cit., pp. 41ff.

26. Compare the reaction of the people on Mount Carmel to the fire of the Lord that consumed Elijah's offering (1 Kings 18:39): 'And when all the people saw it, they fell on their faces; and they said, "The Lord, he is God; the Lord, he is God".' They recognise the work of the Lord, and respond to it; though the verb 'to know' is not used, their situation and response is in effect the same as Jethro's.

27. For this, see W. Zimmerli, 'The Message of the Prophet Ezekiel', in *Interpretation* 23 (1969) 131-157, especially section VIII, pp. 147-149. Zimmerli derives the formula 'and you shall know' (or 'thus you will know') from the legal language of a process of proof (cf. Gen 43:34). This 'recognition formula' is followed by 'I am Yahweh', 'a form of self-presentation by which in encounter an unknown person introduces himself' (cf. Exod 20:2). 'Closer examination shows that the recognition formula always precedes a statement about Yahweh's actions; in our context his judgmental action toward his people. The formula seeks to say that the ultimate meaning of God's action toward his people is to recognise God's revelation in this action. He presents himself to his people in his action as the one he is'.

28. Cf. also Is 49:26.

29. On the large question of revelation through history in the Old Testament, see J. Barr, 'Revelation through History in the Old Testament and Modern Theology,' in *Interpretation* 17 (1963) 193-205 (summarised in G. Fohrer, *Theologische Grundstrukturen des Alten Testaments*, pp. 42-44). Barr argues that in the Old Testament history is not the supreme witness of God's revelation. The Old Testament contains wisdom and liturgical literature as well as 'history', and its 'history' includes much that we would put into other categories. The Old Testament itself, in fact, does not use 'history' as an organising bracket for its material. Barr points rather

to the importance of the idea of 'the word of the Lord' in the Old Testament. This correction of emphasis seems fully justified. See also E. C. Blackman, 'Is History relevant for the Christian Kerygma?', in *Interpretation* 21 (1967) 435-446.

30. Cf. H. W. Robinson, *Redemption and Revelation*, London (1942), p. 165: 'However transcendent God is, the point at which He reveals Himself to us must be a point at which He becomes intelligible to us, that is, a point at which there is kinship between His nature and ours. This is a principle which some theologies have ignored or denied, notably the present day Barthianism.'

THE NEW TESTAMENT CONCEPT OF REVELATION: SOME REFLECTIONS

Sean Freyne

The most intimate truth which this revelation gives us about God and the salvation of man shines forth in Christ, who is himself the mediator and sum-total of Revelation.

VATICAN II CONSTITUTION, *Dei Verbum*, 2.

When what is said in the New Testament is truly heard the concept of revelation in the New Testament meets with the latter's claim to *be* revelation; that is, the New Testament is able to tell us what it understands by revelation only by at the same time asserting that it itself is revelation.

Rudolf Bultmann, 'The New Testament Concept of Revelation', in *Existence and Faith, Shorter Writings*, p. 105

Whether one takes as one's starting point the Christologically inspired Vatican II statement or the Bultmannian notion of God's Word to be encountered in the kerygma, an adequate treatment of the New Testament understanding of revelation would involve writing about the New Testament itself. Nor does the usual approach of investigating the various terms used by different New Testament authors in the hope of arriving at different semantic meanings alleviate the problem. Certainly a good case can be made for distinguishing such terms as *gnorizein*, 'to make known', *apocalyptein*, 'to unveil', *deloun*, 'to indicate' or 'disclose', *phaneroun*, 'to manifest'. An examination of these and other terms in *TDNT* rapidly indicates that different nuances are suggested by each. Yet the truth is that no *one* term established itself, even with any individual New Testament writer, and this suggests that while all are aware of writing from within the fulness of God's final word in Christ, there is no one way in which that reality can be fully expressed or the experience properly articulated. Recent treatments of the concept by systematic theologians are also indicative in that it is frequently suggested that since revelation, described in terms of speech, involves dialogue between God and man, we might take as our starting point *man's* acceptance of an involvement in the divine self-disclosure rather than the more inaccessible notion of *God* addressing us.[1]

In the following reflections we take our cue from these suggestions. Unlike philosophical theology, the Bible never questions the possibility or the fact of God communicating with man. Consequently, rather than surveying the whole field, we have chosen two New Testament witnesses, Mark and John, who, all would agree, are particularly concerned with our topic. We shall ask each of these writers two closely related questions: 1) How does the fulness of revelation unfold itself in the life of Jesus, and 2) how is this perceived from the human side? It would be generally accepted that the two writers reflect very different socio-cultural and theological perspectives, yet we hope to show that their answers to the two questions just posed are strikingly similar. We are not concerned here to argue the case for or against literary dependence between the two works.[2] In fact the overall thesis concerning the nature of revelation that we suggest in this paper is strengthened when no such immediate contacts are presupposed. However, before addressing ourselves to the task just outlined it is necessary to consider the expectation of an end-time revelation in late Judaism. This forms the immediate background for both writers and their readers, and it will help considerably in understanding not just the terminology used by each, but also the conceptual framework within which all New Testament writers approached our topic.

I. THE EXPECTATION OF AN END-TIME REVELATION IN LATE JUDAISM

In his monumental work, *Judentum und Hellenismus*, Martin Hengel has convincingly shown that the quest for a higher wisdom through revelation was a general feature of hellenistic religiosity.[3] Once the cultural wedding of east and west had taken place, the 'rationalism' of classical Greece was soon tempered by the more 'mystical' way of the east. The rise and continued popularity of the mystery religions shows how this search continued in the Roman world despite efforts of Augustus to revive the old national religion of Rome.[4] Judaism could not remain unaffected by these general developments, and without entering into the vexed question of pre-Christian *gnosis*, it is legitimate to see the rise and continued popularity of apocalyptic as the direct outcome of the mood of uncertainty and defensiveness that followed Antiochus IV's reform attempt in 167 BC. Under serious threat from the hellenistic monarchies from without and the hellenisers from within, all branches of Palestinian Judaism became more assertive of its

33

distinctiveness, yet at the same time longed for the finality that would vindicate such claims. In such a climate the stress on special knowledge of the intimate plan of God became a central theme, as different factions of Judaism struggled for supremacy.

Within this social and religious unheaval two different strands of thought dominate late Jewish writing — wisdom and apocalyptic. At first sight they appear directly opposed to each other since the former makes creation the starting point for its reflections about life while the latter lays claim to a special revelation granted to the apocalyptic seer. However, on closer examination surprising similarities of point of view emerge in relation to the subject matter of this paper, and so are worth pursuing further.

(1) Wisdom Personified

The figure of personified wisdom is a constant in all the wisdom books (with the exception of Qoheleth), from the fourth century BC Book of Proverbs to the first century Wisdom of Solomon. It has been suggested that the figure of Wisdom in Prov 8 was conceived as a direct response to that of Job 28, where Wisdom's inaccessibility to all but God himself is stressed.[5] In contrast to this picture, that of Prov 8 paints a highly attractive portrait of Wisdom as the lady who invites all to the banquet of life (9:1-6). Though her pre-existence and closeness to the creator God is stressed, this only serves to underline her importance for man, not her aloofness.[6] Two centuries later Ben Sirach can describe her in terms reminiscent of the Stoic ideas of the world principle, thereby suggesting her universal nature (Sir 24:6-8),[7] but he subsequently identifies her with the 'book of the covenant of the Most High God, the law enjoined by Moses' (24:23). The Alexandrian author of Wisdom of Solomon develops the universal features of wisdom further by envisaging her embracing all the human sciences that were being developed in that cosmopolitan centre (7:17-20).[8] Yet nowhere is her identity with Yahweh, and therefore her rare and special quality, more emphatically declared (vv. 25ff).

As developed in all these books, each in its different cultural and religious setting, the personifield figure of Wisdom enables this tradition as a whole to retain the basic Israelite insight of God's special self-communication to his people, while at the same time abandoning the usual medium of that self-communication, sacred history, for the more universal and all-embracing one of creation. Accordingly, no conflict developed between the rational human starting point of the wisdom movement and the revelational divine character of Israel's life and existence.[9] As already mentioned, the book of Job has most dramatically underlined the hidden nature of Wisdom. Thus Eliphaz sarcastically queries Job: 'Do you listen in on the council of God, and has wisdom been revealed to you?' (15:8). The Yahweh speeches (chs 37—41), with their rhetorical cross-examination of Job to uncover his lack of knowledge, highlight the fact that there is a secret purpose to the universe that lies hidden from man and is known to God alone. While the other wisdom books did not follow this rather daring solution of the problem of man's knowledge of the divine will, the tension between the hiddenness, yet accessibility of Wisdom is maintained by stressing the ethical and religious claims it makes on man. Thus Ben Sirach declares that it is to the humble that God reveals his secrets (Sir 3:19; cf. 4:18; 48:24f). Wisdom is closely allied to prophesy (Sir 24: 33), and Isaiah is an example of the wise man *par excellence* who through a powerful spirit looked into the future and foretold hidden things as yet unfulfilled (Sir 48:25f). Yet human co-operation is also important in the quest for Wisdom since the wise man must devote himself to the study of the law and seek out the hidden meaning of proverbs (Sir 39:1-3). According to Wisdom of Solomon, the wise man by his knowledge of God can claim to be a son of God, and is a reproach to the wicked who seek to destroy him, for 'they do not know the secrets of God nor hope for a recompense of holiness' (2:13-22). Later in the same book every conceivable quality is attributed to Wisdom, again underlining its universalist features in the Diaspora context, yet, 'in each generation she passes into holy souls, making them friends of God and prophets' (7:22f, 27).

In brief, while *wisdom* can be achieved by all, *Wisdom* is the divine self-communication made to those who are open to her invitation and whose lives reflect her values. It is only the wise who can share her spirit and enter into the special relationship with God that she offers. Revelation as Wisdom is both gift and call.

(2) The Apocalyptic Mystery

Recent studies in apocalyptic stress the need for distinguishing between the literary genre Apocalypse and the theological and sociological movement that lies behind such literature.[10] One distinguishing feature of every Apocalypse is the portrayal of a heavenly intermediary who shares a hidden and secret knowledge — usually designated by the word *mysterion* in Greek[11] — with a human recipient. The context of this communication has to do with God's plan for the outcome of history, especially in relation to the just, and it is usually described with vivid imagery. Often the unveiling of the mystery is associated with other features of a visual or auditory nature, sometimes involving a heavenly journey for the recipient and the writing of a message in a scroll or book. Clearly these literary features are intended to convey a sense of special divine communication, irrespective of whether or not ecstatic experiences gave rise to the actual descriptions of the authors.[12]

Despite these very distinctive literary and imaginative features it is remarkable how the pattern already discerned in the wisdom tradition recurs in this body of literature also. Thus, Daniel thanks the God of wisdom for his gift of interpretation and recognises that this is not granted to the non-Israelite wise man (Dan 2:20, 27-29, 47). A foreign king attributes Daniel's powers to 'the spirit of the holy God that is in you' (Dan 4:10). The visions of the second half of the book are intended to console the people of the saints of the Most High (Dan 7:27), who can equally well be described as 'the wise who shall make many understand' (11:23) and who 'will shine like the brightness of the firmament' (12:3). Their wisdom, like that of Daniel's, consists in a strict adherence to the details of the Jewish law and its piety — dietary regulations (Dan 1:8) and prayer (Dan 6:11) — even under the threat of martyrdom. Thus it is possible to detect a real coming together of the wisdom tradition, especially as this had become identified with the torah in Palestinian circles, and apocalyptic as this flourished in the ranks of the *hasidim*.[13]

Similar developments emerge in later Apocalypses and in the Qumran writings that have highly apocalyptic colouring from their background. In 1 Enoch, e.g., Enoch himself is shown the tree of Wisdom of his forefathers (32:3-6), thus suggesting an *Ur-Zeit/End-Zeit* pattern of revelation Yet such knowledge of Wisdom brings its responsibility for the elect, for they will never again sin (5:8). Revelatory language and formulae dominate the closing chapters of this work also.[14] On the basis of his vision the author can 'swear' that the sinner is doomed, but on the contrary, 'blessed are all those who accept the *words of wisdom* and understand them and observe the paths of the Most High and walk in the path of his righteousness (99:10). Thus once again the ethical aspect is heavily stressed, for it is only when behaviour becomes indicative of true understanding that one can speak of the revelation having taken place. At Qumran, the author of the hymns (the teacher of righteousness) repeatedly thanks God for revealing to him his truth or his mysteries (1QH 4:28; 5:11, 25f; 7:26f),[15] yet the community rule makes it clear that the members are those who 'devote themselves to his truth', bringing their strength, their property and their discernment 'so that they can clarify their discernment by the truth of the ordinances of God' (1QS 1:12). While the summary of the community's beliefs in the passage concerning the two spirits (1QS 3:13—4:24) assumes that the spirits of wisdom and folly will contend in the heart of man until the appointed time, it is nevertheless clear that the community does consider itself to be already in possession of the spirit of truth which one can share in by following the ordinances of the community.[16] To conclude this very sketchy outline of late-Jewish apocalyptic thinking about revelation one citation from the late first century BC work II Esdras,[17] reflects best the overall pattern:

> You alone Esra have been *found worthy* to learn this *mystery* of the Most High. Therefore write all these things that you have seen in a book and put them in a secret place. And you shall teach them to *the wise* among the people, whose *hearts* you know are *pure* and can comprehend and keep these *mysteries* (14:6).

Clearly revelation takes place only within the context of human worthiness which manifests itself in actions that correspond to the revelation to be received.

II. THE NEW TESTAMENT UNDERSTANDING
OF THE FULLNESS OF REVELATION

Our investigation of the concept of revelation in late-Judaism as this is expressed in the wisdom literature and the apocalyptic tradition suggest strongly that it is relational in character. Even though both traditions are keenly aware that Wisdom or the disclosure of the divine secrets for history is a God-given gift, they also stress that man's co-operation, especially in relation to his ethical conduct, is an integral part of the revelatory process. The fact that early Christianity as a whole believed that this search for wisdom and revelation had come to an end with the coming of Christ[18] makes our choice of Mark and John all the more interesting. Recent scholarship has spoken of the apocalyptic nature of Mark,[19] whereas the influence of the figure of Wisdom on Johannine thought has also been repeatedly noted.[20] Clearly, neither wisdom nor apocalyptic had lost their significance as useful conceptual frameworks, even with the coming of Christ.

(1) The Apocalyptic Drama, Mark

Recent writing on the gospel of Mark has been particularly concerned with its Christology,[20] and while I am in total agreement that this is indeed the crucial concern of the Evangelist I would argue that for him Christology cannot be understood independently of discipleship – the truth about Jesus emerges in relation to the disciples' varied responses to his actions.[21] A proper understanding of the Christ is not easy, even by the disciple who can be deceived by signs and wonders to worship a false Christ (13:22), never grasping the mystery with which he is entrusted (4:11). What that mystery is emerges only gradually within the Markan drama, and is finally disclosed in the centurion's confession: 'seeing that thus he (Jesus) breathed his last he declared, "truly this man was Son of God" ' (15:39). As has long been recognised, the aura of mystery hangs over the work as a whole, and correspondingly, themes like seeing, hearing, remembering and understanding become the primary challenge of the disciple in the present (cf. 8:14-21). In a word, Mark's drama is one of revelation in which the real struggle is not between Jesus and his opponents, but between Jesus and his disciples who are being invited to discover that the truth about Jesus can only be understood through the cross. Premature proclamation based on the mighty deeds alone only lead to a superficial understanding and will never plumb the depths of the mystery (cf. 1:45; 7:37). Thus after Peter's confession they are strictly charged to keep their insight that Jesus is the Christ to themselves (8:30), and coming down from the mount of transfiguration they are ordered to tell the vision to no man until the Son of Man is raised from the dead (9:9).

This understanding of the overall purpose of Mark's gospel can be illustrated by a number of features of the work as a whole as well as by an examination of individual passages. To begin with the structure suggests a revelational concern. The work is clearly divided into two main parts — 'the book of the mighty deeds' (1:15—8:30) and 'the book of the passion' (8:31—15:39), to apply Dodd's description of the Fourth Gospel to this work. Each section focuses on two very different aspects of the ministry of Jesus, the power and the weakness. Both are climaxed by a confessional statement—Peter's 'You are the Christ' and the centurion's 'Truly this man was Son of God'. Significantly, there is a particular stress on seeing in relation to both statements, with the suggestion that there has been a progression from the first to the second instance.[22] The titles that emerge in these confessions, Christ and Son of God, were combined in the inscription to the whole work at 1:1, thus defining the content of the good news as Mark sees it.[23] Consequently Peter's confession is only partial and in need of deepening through the idea of the suffering Son of man that dominates the second half of the work (8:31; 9:31; 10:33, 45; 14:21, 41). We have already noted that in *Wisdom of Solomon* Wisdom's child calls himself son of God, is resented by his enemies who challenge him to show signs of his Wisdom and is eventually persecuted because of his claims (2:13-20). It could be argued with very good reason that this pattern provides the outline for Mark's story, since ultimately the death of Christ is the result of his adhering to the claim to be God's son (14:61f), a self-understanding that is confirmed by two theophanic declarations: 'You are my son the beloved' (1:11; 9:8).[24] Some commentators have detected a reference to the *'aqedah*, or binding of Isaac in the use of the word *agapetos* in this context. However, in the Jewish tradition that event had revelational overtones also, that would fit in very well with Mark's presentation.[25] The place of Isaac's sacrifice was said to have been Mt Moriah, an old name for Jerusalem, and according to the LXX of Gn 22:14 Abraham called the name of the place 'the Lord appears', a theme further developed in the Targumic tradition where the moment of Isaac's sacrifice was believed to have been accompanied with a heavenly appearance to assure both father and son. There were then good precedents for Mark's linking of sacrifice and revelation by making the cross the moment when the truth about Jesus is perceived by a human for the first time. This is the only 'seeing' that is possible in the present and the elect must wait for confirmation until the return of the victorious Son of Man (13:26) just as he himself had promised before the High Priest (14:62).

Focusing on the parable chapter helps to confirm these impressions that Mark's real concern was a proper understanding of the mystery of Jesus by the disciples. A number of recent studies of the sources of Mark claim that a collection of miracle stories underlies chs 3–5,[26] and presumably the intervening parable chapter is also pre-Markan in some form. This means that the juxtaposing of miracles and parables is due to Markan redaction, thereby suggesting the mysterious nature of the mighty deeds and toning down their wondrous aspect. They are rather signs of Jesus' wisdom, the source of which remains hidden even to his own townspeople just as it did to his relatives and his enemies (3:20-22; 6:2). On the other hand his true relations, the disciples centred on the Twelve have the mystery given to them, but its parabolic, paradoxical nature requires special instruction if they are to grasp its true import. 'Do you not understand this parable? How then will you understand all parables?' (4:13). The parable can be a two-edged sword—either a story full of meaning or the riddle that conceals the truth, but the disciples will have everything explained to them (4:33f). What is given to them is 'the mystery (sing.) of the kingdom of God', which presumably corresponds to 'the gospel of the kingdom' (1:14), which, we have seen, is none other than the person of Jesus as Christ and Son of God (1:1; cf. 8:35; 10:29). Throughout this secret 'apocalypse' in the house there is a constant stress on hearing, heeding, allowing the word to take root and bear fruit, receiving in the measure one gives — all Markan redactional touches to stress the need for active co-operation if the necessary breakthrough in understanding is to be achieved.[27] It should be noted

that the three parables Mark uses in this chapter suit his overall theme perfectly. All three contrast the failure and insignificance of the present with the subsequent unexpected and totally mysterious success in the future. As the process unfolds itself all one can do is trust and wait for the ultimate disclosure which cannot be anticipated.

Looking at Mark's gospel from the perspective of an approach to revelation is therefore quite informative. Though writing in the belief that Jesus' life and death had constituted the eschatological act of God, Mark is keenly aware that that event could be perceived within the present only through a slow and painful process that challenged man at his deepest and most vulnerable level. He consequently presents the ministry of Jesus as a struggle for men's minds while all the time the forces of evil are lurking in the background ready to snatch the word (4:15), or to blind the understanding (*porosis*, 3:5; 6:51; 8:17), or even think purely human thoughts about Jesus and his ministry (8:33). Clearly there is need for purification, even reversal of accepted standards of judging and acting if a real breakthrough is to take place. Thus the chiding question or comment as the disciples fail to grasp the obvious about Jesus in the first half of the work (cf. 4:13, 40; 6:52; 7:18; 8:14-21) gives way to the more gentle tone of the second half, where the disciple is invited to share in the attitude of Jesus—losing his life to save it (8:35), being least of all if he wishes to be greatest (9:35) and becoming servant of all if he wishes to be first (10:43), 'for the Son of Man came not to be served but to serve and to give his life as a ransom for many' (10:45). Thus, understanding and faith are to be elicited by actions rather than words and so the dying and rising Son of Man goes his *way* (10:17) for the ultimate disclosure through death in Jerusalem. Though absent at the crucial moment, the bitter experience of failure, as typified in Peter's denial, can leave them ready for the summons to follow the Risen Lord back to Galilee, there to see him, not as the wonder-working thaumaturg but as the dying and rising Saviour whose life is the ultimate victory over evil.

(2) Incarnate Wisdom: John

As the opening hymn to the *Logos* makes clear, revelation is undoubtedly the central theme of the Fourth Gospel, even if there is no final agreement on the religious milieu in which the unique conception of Jesus' ministry had germinated. As title for the work the Evangelist himself suggests 'the Gospel of Signs', with the concluding statement of purpose: 'Many other signs Jesus did. . . but these are written that you may believe that Jesus is the *Christ*, the *Son of God* and that believing you may have life in his name' (Jn 20:31). Interestingly, these are the

40

two titles that were important for Mark also, and this suggests a similar concern. However, John is not content with traditional titles but fills them with new meaning, or at least brings out their latent content by employing them in a larger framework of the incarnate revealer.[28] We cannot here discuss the mythological background to this presentation—gnostic, sapiential, hermetic, apocalyptic — since clearly for the author of the Fourth Gospel the important thing is the understanding of Jesus' life that he wishes to convey, namely that he is the end-time Revealer. Therefore the author presses Christology into the service of his overall purpose and stresses the unique union between Jesus and God as the warrant that he is indeed what he claims to be. While the prologue sets the tone in this regard with its doctrine of the pre-existent *Logos*— reminiscent of the pre-existent Wisdom[29]—becoming incarnate (1:1, 14), the same concern runs through the whole work. There is identity of function between Jesus and God in regard to judgment and power over life, since 'the Father works until now and I work' (5:17). This means that he shares the Father's name (5:43; 17:11), has power over all things (3:35; 13:3) and has life in himself just as the Father has (5:26). This union of Father and Son is both moral and mystical. Jesus' work is to do the will of him who sent him, a theme that is repeated many times throughout the work.[30] As a result he can speak of a total union between them based on mutual love and indwelling (10:38; 14:10f; 17:21-23; 3:35; 5:20; 10:17). The only work that Jesus has to do is to make known the Father's name (17:6). Thus the term *logos* with semitic resonances of *dabar*—word *and* event—is most appropriate to express John's central thought: 'The *words* that I say to you I do not speak on my own authority, but the Father who dwells in me is doing his *works*' (14:10). Significantly, Jesus declares that doing this work is his food (4:31), since in ch. 6 he repeatedly identifies himself as the bread of life for the believers in his role as revealer, thus using an image that is also used for Wisdom (cf. e.g. Sir 24:21f), both for his relation to the Father and the believers relation to him. Indeed all the images used for Jesus and his work in this gospel—Son of Man, shepherd, light, water, have definite revelational overtones, all leading to the clear statement: 'I am the way and the truth and the life' (14:6). Correspondingly, the hiddenness and inaccessability of God are highlighted: no man has ever seen God (1:18), and so the Jews who do not believe are told: 'his voice you have never heard, his form you have never seen and you do not have his word abiding in you' (5:37f). As the Revealer, Jesus alone can bridge the knowledge-gap between God and man.

In presenting the mysterious Messiah Mark had to stress the need for the Christian disciple to be drawn into the mystery of Jesus in order to understand it properly. Seeing the truth about Jesus from the vantage point of the cross demanded looking to the future to see the coming Son of Man as the confirmation of seeing him in Galilee in the present. Given the often repeated declaration of the purpose of Jesus' coming and the identity of his person as the Revealer it might come as some surprise that John too has to underline the challenge to understanding that this revelation poses, even for those who are well disposed towards Jesus. The failure of those who do not come to the light is described in many different ways: their works are evil (3:19); they have neither the word nor the love of God in them (5:38, 42); they judge according to the flesh (8:15); they are of the world or from below (8:23); they cannot bear to hear his words because they are of their father, the devil (8:43f); they do not know God (8:55); they do not belong to Jesus' sheep (10:26) and ultimately, with typical Johannine irony, they preferred the honour (*doxa*) of men to the glory (*doxa*) of God (12:43). On examination these reasons for the Jewish failure to believe have both a religious and an ethical character. Moral failure that does not wish to have itself exposed is one reason for ignoring the claim of Jesus, but even more significant is the failure to have a basic openness to the truth and the longing for it—the predisposition that corresponds to revelation itself, yet determines the subsequent understanding and acceptance of it: 'Everyone who is of (*ek* of origin or source) the truth hears my voice' (18:36).

What of others? How in the Johannine perspective do disciples and those who are not ill-disposed come to a knowledge of the truth? First of all the Spirit is particularly important for the Johannine church. He is the Spirit of truth (14:16) with a twofold function: that of Paraclete or Advocate/Consoler for the church in a hostile world and the one who leads them into all truth.[31] He comes in Jesus' name and brings to their remembrance all that Jesus had said to them. The things which Jesus cannot say he will present to them later, for he simply speaks what he hears and presents it to them (14:26; 16:12-15). As such he replaces the returning Son of Man of Mark as the eschatological vindicator of those who believe in the present, for at his coming he will convince the world of sin, of righteousness and of judgment (16:8). Thus while the Johannine church is deeply conscious of living within the fulness of the *eschaton*, the Spirit is still necessary for it to continue to understand the meaning of God's final Word. The Spirit's role of calling to mind all that Jesus had spoken (14:26) would appear to be particularly important in view of the stress on this very activity of remembering on the part of the disciples at the beginning and end of the 'Book of the Signs' (2:22; 12:16). Clearly, the disciples grasped the full meaning of Jesus' life only through a long process of Spirit-filled reflection in the post-Easter situation.[32]

Another aspect of John's overall presentation that points in the same direction is his theory of signs in relation to Jesus' ministry. Thus, when Jesus' life was eventually perceived to have been the revelation of the Father's glory this was understood to have taken place in signs (2:11; 4:54; 6:26; 11:47; 20:30), thereby highlighting the tension between revelation as event and the human understanding of its significance. The Johannine community was well aware that the revelation that took place in Jesus was of its very nature a veiled one, 'in the flesh' (1:14), and so demanded faith from those who would see its true significance. Thus the Jesus of the signs in John has a similar function to Jesus the mysterious messiah in Mark in relation to the believers' response. Both images are a summons to faith rather than an irrefutable proof of identity. That is why it is possible in John, just as in Mark, for a super-ficial understanding of Jesus to emerge, based on these very actions. This can be characterised as a human way of seeing and judging, as the examples of Nicodemus (2:23—3:1),[33] the Galilean crowds (6:26) and the brothers of the Lord (7:1-3) clearly demonstrate. The signs are thereby reduced to 'signs that are equal to wonders' (*semeia kai terata*, 4:48), and cannot function as true pointers to the reality of Jesus. All the Johannine signs are placed in the first half of the work (chs 2—12), that is *before* the hour of Jesus has come (cf. 2:4; 7:30; 8:20). At the end of the series his hour is solemnly said to have arrived, and it is now defined as the hour of his glorification (12:23, 27; 13:31; 17:1), or the hour of his going from this world to the Father (13:1). In other words, in his presentation of the ministry of Jesus, John, like Mark, sets up a deliberate tension between the actual glorification of Jesus which is the moment of the community's real breakthrough in understanding, as Jesus himself had predicted (3:14f; 6:62; 8:28), and those 'remembered' episodes which can *now, from the vantage point of the hour of glorifi-cation,* be seen as signs of that same glory present in Jesus.[34] While Mark sees the cross as the final reversal of all human values and stand-ards and John regards it as the moment of victory, both can treat it as the vital breakthrough point in terms of understanding the revelation of God in Jesus, without which the remainder of his life would remain shrouded in mystery. For John the community cannot expect such signs of Jesus' glory to continue, and hence the need for the Evangelist to make his selection and present them in writing for his readers so that others too can believe. Unlike Thomas, their faith must be based on the word of the preaching, now committed to writing (cf. 3:11; 19:35), but such faith is declared particularly blessed: 'Blessed are they Thomas, who have not seen and have believed' (2):29).[35] It is to such believers that the so-called 'farewell discourses' are directed promising a new form of revelation as they live their life in the unbelieving world: 'Anyone who receives my commandments and keeps them will be the one who loves me; and anyone who loves me will be loved by my Father, and I shall love him and *manifest* myself to him' (14:21). Love replaces the various signs as the ultimate experience of God's presence in Jesus for the community, and gives them a glimpse of the mystery that is God (cf. 1 Jn 4:7-16).[36]

Conclusion

Our exploration of the way in which two New Testament writers deal with the idea of revelation, when judged against the late-Jewish background, suggests a number of important themes for contemporary theology.

1. Revelation is an eschatological gift, and consequently no Christian theology should ignore the category 'future' in its attempt to explicate the concept. The blending of wisdom and apocalyptic in the late Jewish period and the use of the coming Son of Man and the gift of the Spirit by Mark and John all suggest that man is constantly in the role of waiting for revelation, even when that is believed to have already taken place.

2. Man's waiting expresses itself in terms of his ethical behaviour, since it is to the wise that Wisdom is given and the secrets are disclosed to the just. For Mark suffering discipleship is the way to understand a suffering Messiah, while John emphasises that love of the brother 'as I have loved you' will bring about a true manifestation of Father and Son to the believers and a recognition that God is love.

3. This suggests that revelation can only happen for those who have already received it. There is a real paradox here, but both Mark and John in their different ways are clearly aware of the truth of that paradox. The former uses a piece of popular wisdom, 'to him who has more will be given', in the context of instruction to disciples concerning the mystery that has been given to them, and tha latter accuses the Jews of not receiving Jesus, the Word of God, because they have not the word of God in them. It does not occur to either writer to question the logic of this, nor do problems of later theology about human freedom and divine predestination present themselves, for each is overwhelmingly convinced that revelation is God's gift of himself which is freely given to his own. It is not for man to question the mode of the giving but to gratefully accept the gift.

4. This does not reduce man to a passive recipient however. Revelation must be capable of being expressed as truth or wisdom before it can be said to have occured. Since it is to man that God reveals himself, his revelation does not exist in a vacuum but only in people. Ultimately, God can only reveal himself through the human, and this is as true of the climactic moment of the divine self-disclosure as it is of any other. That is why the two Christian writers we have examined, even though writing from the fulness of an Easter vision, present the climax of revelation in Jesus as the mystery that is parable or the wisdom that is sign.

NOTES

1. K. Rahner, art. 'Revelation', in *Sacramentum Mundi*, Herder, 1970, vol. 5, 348-53; J. P. Mackey, *The Problem of Religious Faith*, Dublin Helicon, 1972, 113-211. For a brief but informative summary of recent Protestant approaches cf. J. Barr, art. 'Revelation as History', in *IDB* suppl. vol. 746-49, challenging the usefulness of this particular approach that has become very popular in post-war biblical theology.
2. A number of very interesting structural and thematic, as distinct from traditional, similarities emerge and are pointed out in passing. I hope to develop these in a more formal way elsewhere as they seem to confirm Lightfoot's astute observation, 'A Consideration of three Markan passages', in *In Memoriam E. Lohmeyer*, Stuttgart 1951, 115, that every theological idea that is rough-hewn in the gospel of Mark appears finely honed in John.
3. *Judentum und Hellenismus*, Tubingen, Mohr, 2nd ed. 1973, Excursus 4, 'Weisheit durch Offenbarung als Wesenmerkmal spatantiker Religiositat', 381-93.
4. A. D. Nock, *Conversion. The Old and the New in Religion from Alexander the Great to Augustine of Hippo*, Oxford, Univ. Press, Paperbacks, 1972, 99-137.
5. Hengel, *Jud. und Hell.* 275-82.
6. R. N. Whybray, *Wisdom in Proverbs. The Concept of Wisdom in Proverbs 1−9*, Studies in Biblical Theology, first series 45, London S.C.M., 1965, 76-94.
7. Hengel, *Jud. und Hell.*, 288f.
8. J. M. Reese, *Hellenistic Influences in the Book of Wisdom and its Consequence*, Analecta Biblica 41, Rome 1970.
9. Hengel, *Jud. und Hell.*, 299, attributes the first attempts to combine reason and revelation to the Alexandrian Jew, Aristobulus, a near contemporary of Ben Sirach.
10. Cf. J. J. Collins, 'Apocalypse: Towards the Morphology of a genre', with bibliography in *S.B.L. Seminar Papers, 1977*, ed. P. J. Achtemeier, Miss. Mont. Scholars Press, 359-370.
11. Cf. R. E. Brown, *The Semitic Background to the Term Mystery in the New Testament*, Facet Books, Bib. ser. 21, Philadelphia, Fortress

Press 1967, 2ff, gives a good summary of the linguistic usage. Cf. also G. Bornkamm, art. 'Mysterion', *TDNT*, IV, 802-828 for details.

12. Hengel, *Jud. und Hell.*, 376f, does not exclude the possibility of such ecstatic experiences on the basis of comparative religious experiences in the hellenistic ethos.

13. Hengel, *Jud. und Hell.*, 369ff.

14. Cf. the careful literary and thematic study of these chapters by G. W. Nickelsburg, 'The Apocalyptic Message of 1 Enoch 92–105', *CBQ* 39 (1977) 309-28.

15. J. Murphy-O'Connor, 'Truth: Paul and Qumran' in *Paul and Qumran*, ed. J. Murphy-O'Connor, London, Chapman 1968, 179-230, esp. 182-86; O. Betz, *Offenbarung und Schriftauslesung in der Qumransekte*, Tubingen, Mohr, 1960, 54f, notes that these not merely include the law as interpreted by the community but also other hidden things such as rituals and practices that were an important part of the community's way of life (1QS 5:10f; CD 3:13-15).

16. O. Betz, *Offenbarung und Schriftauslesung*, 143-51, esp. 147f, notes that in this passage the doctrine of the two spirits replaces the more usual understanding of the spirit as revealer, but the strong ethical colouring of the conception removes the apparent inconsistency in the community's doctrine of the spirit. J. H. Charlesworth, 'A Critical Comparison of the Dualism of IQS 3:13–4:26 and the Dualism contained in the Fourth Gospel', *NTS* 15 (1969) 389-418, esp. 395-402, also notes the special features of the doctrine of the spirit in this passage and speaks of a modified cosmic dualism between the two spirits, since both are clearly subordinated to the one God and the spirit of perversity has a finite existence, appearing after God and destined to be destroyed before the end.

17. This Apocalypse is to be dated after the fall of Jerusalem in 70 C.E., probably under Domitian, according to O. Eissfeldt, *The Old Testament. An Introduction*, English trans. Oxford, Blackwell, 1965, 624ff. It belongs therefore to the same generation as Mark and John.

18. In support of this one can point to the strong influence of Wisdom on Q, as has been pointed out by e.g. J. M. Robinson, *'Logoi Sophon*: On the *Gattung* of Q', in *The Future of our Religious Past. Essays in Honour of Rudolf Bultmann* (English version) ed. J. M. Robinson, New York, Harper and Row, 1971, 84-130, and more recently, 'Jesus as *Sophos* and *Sophia*: Wisdom Tradition and the Gospels', in *Aspects of Wisdom in Judaism and Early Christianity*, ed. R. L. Wilkin, University of Notre Dame Press, 1975, 1-16. On Jesus' own background cf. N. Perrin, 'Wisdom and Apocalyptic in the Message of Jesus', in *Proceedings of the Society of Biblical Literature*, ed. L. C. McCaughey, 1972, 1, 543-572.

19. N. Perrin, e.g. *The New Testament. An Introduction*, New York, Harcourt Brace and Jovanovich, 1974, 143-66, describes Mark as 'The Apocalyptic Drama'. On the wisdom influences in John, cf. *inter multos*, R. E. Brown, *The Gospel According to John*, The Anchor Bible 29, New York, Doubleday, 1966, cxxii-v, with bibliography.

20. Cf. e.g. T. Weeden, *Mark: Traditions in Conflict*, Philadelphia, For-

tress Press 1971; N. Perrin, in *Christology and a Modern Pilgrimage. A Discussion with Norman Perrin*, ed. H. D. Betz, Claremont Univ. Press, 1971, 1-71; H. C. Kee, *Community of the New Age. Studies in Mark's Gospel*, Philadelphia, Westminster, 1977, esp. ch. 5.

21. Cf. my *The Twelve: Disciples and Apostles. An Introduction to the Theology of the First Three Gospels*, London, Sheed & Ward, 1968, 106-50; E. Best, 'The Role of the Disciples in Mark', *NTS* 23 (1977) 377-401; P. S. Minear, 'Audience Criticism and Markan Ecclesiology' in *Neues Testament und Geschichte. Festschrift Oscar Cullmann*, Tubingen, Mohr, 1972, 79-90.

22. Contrast the following: 8:11-14 and 15:32, the enemies of Jesus ask for a sign to be convinced; 8:22-6 and 10:46-52, sight-giving miracles, with the second leading to discipleship; 8:18 a question put to the disciples about seeing and hearing and 15:39, a statement that the centurion saw; 13:26; 14:62; 16:7, all referring to various future seeings as a vindication for the claims of the present.

23. The word *euaggelion* is a key word for Mark as is defined in terms of the Christology at 8:35 and 10:29, in that losing one's life or leaving all for the sake of Jesus or for the sake of the gospel can be equiparated. Cf. in particular W. Marxsen, *Der Evangelist Markus*, Gottingen, 1959, 83-92; R. Schnackenburg, 'Das Evangelium im Verstandnis des altesten Evangelisten' in *Orientierung an Jesus. Zur Theologie der Synoptiker*, ed. P. Hoffmann, Freiburg, Herder, 1973, 309-24, esp. 317f.

24. Cf. in this regard the suggestive comments of K. Berger, 'Die koniglichen Messiastraditionen des Neuen Testaments', *NTS* 20 (1973) 1-44, esp. 28-37.

25. Thus E. Best, *The Temptation and the Passion. The Markan Soteriology*, Cambridge Univ. Press, S.N.T.S. Monographs 2, 1965, 167-73, with reference to the study of G. Vermes, *Scripture and Tradition in Judaism*, Leiden 1961, 204-22; cf. also R. le Deaut, *La Nuit Paschale*, Analecta Biblica, 22, Rome, PIB Press, 1963, 133-213; F. Lentzen-Deis, *Die Taufe Jesu nach den Synoptikern*, Frankfurter Theologishe Studien 4, Frankfurt, Knecht, 1970, esp. 195-248, calls the Baptism narrative a 'Deute-Vision', 'interpretative vision' on the basis of the Targums of Gn 22. R. Daly, 'The Soteriological Significance of the Sacrifice of Isaac' *CBQ* 39 (1977) 45-75, esp. 68-71 dealing with Mark, but without reference to the revelatory aspects of the sacrifice.

26. Thus, e.g. L. Keck, 'Mk 3:7-12 and the Markan Christology', *JBL* 84 (1965) 341-58; P. J. Achtemeier, 'Towards the Isolation of a pre-Markan Miracle Catena', *JBL* 89 (1970) 265-91, and 'The Origin and Function of the pre-Markan Catena', *JBL* 91 (1972) 198-221.

27. Q. Quesnell, *The Mind of Mark. Interpretation and Method through the Exegesis of Mk 6:52*, Analecta Biblica 38, Rome, PIB Press, 1964, esp. 72-87 and 209-221, has a detailed redactional study of this chapter. Cf. also J. Lambrecht, 'Redaction and Theology in Mark IV', in *L'Evangile selon Marc. Tradition et Redaction*, ed. M. Sabbe, Bibliotheca ETL xxxiv, Leuven Univ. Press, Gembloux 1974, 269-307. Recent writing on the literary genre parable also stresses

their metaphorical nature; cf. e.g. in relation to Mark, M. Boucher, *The Mysterious Parable. A Literary Study*, CBQ Monograph series 6, 1977.

28. G. McRae, 'The Fourth Gospel and *Religionsgeschichte'*, *CBQ* 32 (1970) 13-26, makes the helpful suggestion that the variety of Christological titles used by the author, e.g. in 1:19-51, is his way of incorporating all the current labels in the church even though none of them corresponds adequately with the author's own model.

29. R. Brown, *The Gospel According to John*, I, Appendix 2, esp. 521-3, favours the view that there is a strong wisdom influence in John's portrayal of the *logos*, following the parallels set out by C. H. Dodd, *The Interpretation of the Fourth Gospel*, Cambridge Univ. Press, 1953, 274ff. R. Bultmann, 'Die Religionsgeschichtliche Hintergrund des Prologs Zum Johannesevangelium' in *Studia Exegetica*, I, Tubingen, Mohr, 1967, 10-35, argues that the Prologue follows the pattern of Wisdom as this is described in 1 Enoch 42:1-2: Wisdom could find no dwelling place among men, and so returned to her place in heaven.

30. He has not come of his own accord or on his own authority (7:28; 8:42; 5:43); he acts on his Father's instructions, speaking only the words the Father has given him (5:19f; 12:49; 14:10; 17:8, 14). Cf. R. Bultmann, *Theology of the New Testament*, 2 vols., English trans. London, SCM 1965, 2, 49ff.

31. R. Brown, *The Gospel According to John*, 2, Appendix v, 'The Paraclete', 1135-43.

32. Cf. F. Mussner's interesting study based on what he calls the gnosiological terms of the Fourth Gospel, *The Historical Jesus and the Fourth Gospel*, Quaestiones Disputatae, English trans. Herder, London, 1965.

33. Note the emphasis on the term *anthropos* 'man' in these verses, and cf. Mk 7:8; 8:27, 33.

34. C. H. Dodd, *Interpretation*, 383, (cf. also 439), puts the point well: 'In principle the Christ of the Book of Signs is the Christ who dies and rises again... The works of Christ are all 'signs' of his finished work. The signs are true provided that he who works them is the Son of Man who was exalted and glorified through the cross.'

35. R. Fortna, 'The Fourth Gospel's portrayal of Jesus' signs: Source and Redaction', *JBL* 89 (1970) 151-66, especially 162f, on believing and not seeing in the Johannine perspective.

36. C. H. Dodd, *Interpretation*, 398f, points out the significance of the change in vocabulary between the Book of the Signs and these Discourses. *Agape* and *agapan* occurs 32x in the latter and 6x in the former; *zoe* and its derivatives occurs 50x in the former and 6x in the latter.

MODERN THEOLOGY AND REVELATION

Míceál Ledwith

1. AN HISTORICAL PERSPECTIVE

In the late eighteenth century the first signs appeared of an escape from the rationalism which would have admitted an historical revelation merely as a necessary cultural prelude to humanity's achievement of a purified religion of reason. This liberation resulted largely from the theology of history elaborated by Johann Gottfried Herder and the emphasis on experience in the work of Friedrich Schleiermacher. Herder was the father of a line of thought that descended through Hegel and Schelling, the Salvation History School and Dilthey's philosophy, and which has revived in a very modified way in the German 'Revelation as History' movement.

The giants of this debate in the present century were unquestionably Barth, Brunner, Tillich and Bultmann, and, however unfashionable the topic of revelation was in Protestantism when Richard Niebuhr wrote, the great contributions of these four men in the twenty years that followed the publication of his book placed the subject at the forefront of Protestant theological concern. The topic deserved that place since perhaps no other area of theology has had so much to absorb in terms of gain from the recovery of Scripture and the great discoveries in Ancient Near Eastern archaeology and comparative religion. Some of this recovered information actually seemed to threaten many of the traditional ways of thinking about Divine Revelation, and its relation to Scripture, particularly, in a way that has been without parallel for many centuries. However the individual theologies of Barth and Bultman may differ from one another their notion of revelation as a kerygma without history was as unacceptable to the Revelation as History School as it was previously to men such as Cullmann and Althaus. Barth's antithesis between Revelation and history fitted well with his idea of a transcendent Revelation located in the area of 'pre-History' (*Urgeschichte*) while Bultmann fled with Revelation into the sphere of *Geschichtlichkeit* ('existential meaning in the history of the individual'): a refuge from

49

the godless cause of 'objective history'. This is quite close to the sharp distinction Niebuhr had made between 'external history' as an objective area, and 'internal history' as a subjectivist evaluation. This effects a division between history as a positivistic science and faith as a subjective attitude.

Within Roman Catholic theology at the same period, Revelation was generally seen as a message from God to man: an intervention by God through events and their prophetic interpretations, eventually through Christ, showing in a concealed way certain truths that belonged to the supernatural order. Niebuhr's understanding of Revelation would have appeared to this tradition as at best anthropomorphic or naturalistic with God added as an afterthought. This particular tradition of a division of truth into natural and divine in almost exclusivist terms would probably be more difficult to locate before the early part of the Middle Ages, when it was hoped that most of what faith held about God could be illuminated by an approach from the side of human knowledge. The standard Catholic view of Revelation prior to Vatican II was largely due to the influence of St Augustine and medieval scholasticism which pictured revelation in terms of a master-pupil relationship. For St Thomas, Revelation resembled a divinely-given supplement to philosophy. This trend developed further under the pressures of the Reformation when the stress was shifted from the authority of God to that of the Church seen as revealed truth's custodian.

The first signs of renewal in the Catholic Theology of Revelation came in the late nineteen forties, and seem to have been due principally to the upsurge in biblical studies after *Divino Afflante Spiritu*, coupled with a need felt of relating revelation theology to preaching, and to the patristic and medieval theological traditions. The reviving Protestant tradition of the time also helped this renewal as did the contemporary philosophical currents such as evolutionism and phenomenology. These new movements were not greeted with enthusiasm at first, but in *Dei Verbum* one sees the biblical and personalist viewpoint in the ascendent in its understanding of revelation as more a 'communication of life' than primarily of doctrine. There is no way in which propositional dogmatic theology is to be downvalued but in *Dei Verbum* it is seen as a product of the relationship between God and man.

After Vatican II the development continued in Catholic theology, the first really significant work to appear being Rene Latourelle's *The Theology of Revelation* (1966) which placed the category of historical events at the centre of understanding of revelation. Latourelle felt that no event in human history was so outstanding as to be automatically authenticated as an instance of divine revelation: together with the

50

event an interpreter enjoying an interior divine illumination is needed to grasp its significance. This same trend was followed by H. R. Schlette (*Epiphany as History* [1969]) who seems to maintain that the true significance of historical fact can be known only in faith, but he does not provide any significant explanation of how one is to understand the source of faith in this perspective. Another writer strongly emphasising the presence of revelation in contemporary life is Gabriel Moran in his difficult book *The Present Revelation* (1972) in which the argument of his earlier *The Theology of Revelation* is brought to its conclusion. There is a single revelation and a multitude of ways in which it is grasped. The revelation in Jesus was unique because of the degree of his receptivity to God's message.

The giants of this period have been Barth and Brunner. The Revelation as History School has provided the first real alternative to these theologies in Protestantism, radically proposing that the events of experience are the acknowledged source of faith even though God may remain as hidden as revealed in these events. In passages from *Dei Verbum* the insistence is clear that Christ is the meaning of all history, including our inner history and experience. This has affinities with other theologies of revelation in Protestantism and Anglicanism, such as those of Niebuhr, Alan Richardson and Van Harvey. It is not always easy to discern behind a superficial similarity if there is real agreement on basic issues, but if these theologians were to clarity their ambiguity on the central question in revelation theology—whether human reason ever can grasp the divine in an authentic although imperfect word — then we could feel that the fundamental concept of revelation they held was not essentially at variance with the message of *Dei Verbum*.

Paradoxically, more extreme views have been propounded within Roman Catholicism, for instance in *The Present Revelation*, already noted and in J. P. Mackey's *The Problems of Religious Faith* (1972). Mackey concludes his penetrating analysis by voicing unhappiness that theologians continue to use the term 'revelation' as a key word and foundational theological concept. He argues that we should abandon the use of the word 'revelation' in this sense and replace it by 'faith' for it is faith, he feels, that gives rise to expectations of revelation.

Since the time of Schleiermacher there has been a tendency in the mainstream of theology to downgrade the rational element in faith and also to view revelation as the product of an attitude of faith rather than as something derived under God's inspiration from the meditation of reason on history. The most striking instance of this is probably Bultmann's idea that the kergymatic significance of what is believed is not necessarily tied to what basis it might have in historical fact. This esti-

51

mate of revelation ultimately can be traced to Kant's division of reality and value and to the influence of Kierkegaard and Wilhelm Herrmann. It seems to me that this is the tradition in which Mackey's work stands, as do similar recent contributions in the same field. I do not wish to diminish the contribution this book has made on a very tortured topic, but some aspects that it treats are worthy of further attention, particularly the abandonment of revelation as a foundational theological concept. This seems perilously close to what Richard Niebuhr was writing about thirty years ago when he spoke about 'external' and 'internal' history. Mackey's position seems to reduce faith to a subjective stance, and uncomfortably would seem to estimate history as a positivistic science. Here we are back again with the perennial debates on the relationship of faith and reason: apart from all the other difficulties in this field a major problem for some time has been the variety of ways in which the terms themselves have been defined. The unfortunate side effect of this tradition from the time of Schleiermacher is that there is really nothing any longer to distinguish faith from an interpretative bias which may not be able, as a result, to vindicate its claims very successfully against rival theistic interpretations, not to speak of those that may be agnostic, nihilist or atheistic. If it is maintained that the statements of theology are essentially insupportable by reason's grasp on history, the inevitable reaction will be that such statements need not be taken very seriously even if some sort of *a posteriori* verification should be admitted.

What I have dealt with so far are *consequences* of such an estimate of faith and revelation and I think they are consequences of which we must be aware before we adopt the main premises. However, there are other reasons why the isolation of faith as a unique approach to reality cannot be maintained in such stark terms. In popular debate religious belief is often contrasted with that paradigm of respectable knowledge —scientific statements. Sometimes they are even contrasted as superstition versus truth. The caricature of science in use here is that of a supremely confident and objectively based study. The same type of contrast on a more sophisticated plane can be seen occasionally in the philosophers' of language division between religious beliefs (as noncognitive language) and empirically verifiable knowledge; and in the existentialist tradition's division between 'nature' and 'history'. More modern insights into the nature of scientific knowledge show that it is fundamentally based on tentative postulates and working models that try to express inadequately that which eludes objective and totally adequate expression. In scientific knowledge there is always an interaction between experience and interpretation; there is always a usage of mental constructs or models, and there is a significant community role both in adopting and rejecting paradigms of acceptable explanations. In this light the radical dichotomy between the language of religion and of science, even on the grounds of the uniqueness of its approach to reality, can hardly be sustained.

I am not denying in any way, naturallly, that faith is the gift of the Spirit of God and not a product of reason, but I would like to keep distinct the narrow area of rational certainty from the much more broad area of rationality. Even if we realise that faith cannot be the product of reason, that should not affect the fact that we would prefer the knowledge of historical revelations to be logically prior. I think it would be unfortunate to say we are not concerned with the truth of faith but only with its meaning, for the claim of meaning has to be referred in the last analysis to the historical events faith statements claim to transmit. Mackey tries to save revelation from its fate at the hands of a crude philosophy of history, but I do not think it is necessary to sacrifice faith in the process by reducing it to a matter of religious psychology.

II. REFLECTIONS

Some theologians see themselves faced by stark alternatives at the present stage in the development of the theology of revelation. If revelation cannot be manifested either in a crudely objective way through historical events, or given by the interior illumination of a prophet, then they feel that 'revelation' can no longer be sustained as a real category in theology but should be replaced by 'faith'. I would consider that these are not the alternatives that follow, even having recognised the likelihood of the hidden character of God's action in the world. What gives trouble here is a presupposition about the nature of human knowing of which we may not always be conscious. Theologians who think in this way seem to be working with a theory of knowledge based on what Popper used to call 'the bucket theory of the mind' (*Objective Knowledge*, p. 60). This is expressed more elegantly in philosophical terms by saying that the mind is a *tabula rasa* on which the senses engrave their messages. The central idea is that all experience consists of information received through the senses. Working with this presupposition of how knowledge is formed you would have to envisage revelation as a message from God objectively and startlingly made present in events or whatever, in order to retain it as a valid theological idea. If this is not verified then we would be driven to say it is useless to talk about revelation at all. A more realistic epistemology, it seems to

me, will realise that all human knowledge is 'dispositional and exspecta-
tional' as Popper says, and that our 'senses are theory impregnated'. In
short there is no sense organ in which modes of anticipation are not
already inbuilt by nature, so that there is an immense personal contribution of the subject in all forms of human knowing. This is not the
place to go into further detail on this matter but I think the failure of
the 'bucket theory' is clear as is the failure of all other theories which
attempt to trace our knowledge totally to observations or to what is
put into the organism. It seems more accurate to say that what is
ignored or seen, or what is recognised as relevant, depends very considerably on the innate structure of the subject. On this understanding
of human knowledge and how it develops, an objective revelation is
very much an idea which can be retained without replacing it in its
foundational theological position by the concept of faith.

I also wonder if such views of faith as I have criticised do not make
revelation very much a cerebral thing, to do with information and
knowledge as the antidote of ignorance. While not wishing to under-
value in the slightest way the importance of this element in revelation
we can question its predominance both on the grounds of common-
sense and on how it squares with the biblical data. We have never really
recovered from the *Critique of Pure Reason*. The question of how we
know becomes the dominant question, and religious knowledge the area
of central concern. A recent book by Gordon Kaufman, *God the
Problem*, is fascinated by this aspect of the question of God which has
reached its highest level in Barth. If we define revelation in this Platonic
way as the communication of knowledge of God primarily through the
person of Jesus Christ we may find ourselves in serious difficulty. A just
account of the Old Testament may be found difficult, the message of
Jesus is diminished, and we find ourselves trying to achieve a truce in
the battle between Christianity and the other major religions. If we
choose to define the uniqueness of Jesus in terms of revealing *knowledge* of God, then we will logically have to deny that God reveals
knowledge of himself elsewhere, and we will also fail to do justice to
the fulness of Chirst. Man's great difficulty is not ignorance: we have
long realised that virtue is not knowledge. Man's primary difficulties are
imcompletion, evil, wrongdoing and guilt, all benefits of a divided
nature. If our difficulty were merely ignorance then revealed *knowledge*
would relieve the situation, but if our real difficulty is the evil a divided
nature brings (as Genesis said) then a strong emphasis on regaining
wholeness, on forgiveness and reconciliation, must be found in our idea
of God's revelation. Jesus the Revealer of God was above all the Saviour
and Healer and I think it is here we will find his unique role in relation

54

to men. It is here we can locate the primary significance of the Incarnation and its continuation in the Church's sacramental system. The question of knowledge of God is of course also a very serious one for modern theology, but I think that there has been a tendency in the modern theology of revelation to confine itself to the epistemological track with a corresponding neglect of such questions as I have outlined above. In a time of systematisation and academic reflection there is always a tendency to make religion a cerebral affair (we saw it in a unique way in Gnosticism), and I think there is a similar fixation in this area of theology today.

III. THE MODE OR PROCESS OF REVELATION

A crucial question in the theology of revelation concerns the way in which God gave it to man. Most recent treatments of revelation either have not devoted much attention to this aspect of the question or have deduced conclusions that seem utterly alien to the traditional persuasion concerning God's revealing acts in the world. The area of the 'how' or 'process' of revelation is not an easy one to approach since it is hedged about with suspicions and is full of pitfalls for the unwary. Nevertheless, in a sense this is the most important aspect of the question for it sheds a great deal of light on exactly what our Christian beliefs are, to speak positively. Negatively, a false conception of the process by which God showed himself can engender false expectations, not alone concerning the nature of his action in the period of foundational revelation, but also in relation to how one might find him in the world today. This can corrupt our idea of God and since this is the central dogmatic affirmation, a misunderstanding here will eventually make its influence felt in all other areas of dogmatic belief and moral understanding. Frequently it is people working with an idea of God that is too slavishly anthropomorphic, even bordering on the crude and superstitious, who come to believe they must reject belief in religion as part of the process of their growth to maturity. Very often, even among the most sincere believers, God is considered to have acted in a way more resembling the crude interruptive acts to which a human revealer would be limited, rather than in a way more consonant with his role as Creator. Obviously the 'interventions' of a Creator will be radically different in kind from those produced by a creature. If this basic fact were recognised a lot of difficulties in understanding the process of revelation would be considerably lessened.

It is now commonplace to realise that God's revealed truths were not given to mankind instantly and fully-formed, but that they were deliver-

55

ed gradually and through a painful process of moral revelation and awareness. In fact it seems reasonably clear that one can only understand and accept a picture of God that is not too remotely beyond your own moral horizon. This should always have been obvious for if God were to do other than reveal in this way he would have to by-pass the whole creation process of growth and development which he had previously set in motion and so carefully nurtured down the ages.

Even a glimpse at the record of revelation given to the Hebrews clearly shows us traces of belief in a savage type of God akin to El at the very early chronological beginnings of the Old Testament. Some of the more obvious examples of this are of course in Exodus 4:24-26 (Yahweh and Moses on Mt Sinai); 2 Sam 6:4-8 (The slaying of Uzzah for a well-intentioned act with a good reason); Psalm 78:65 (God likened to a man rising from a drunken stupor to kill his enemies); or even in the closing vindictive verses of that most irenic Good Shepherd Psalm. A God of that moral quality is not surprisingly a reflection of the stage of moral awareness of his people, and this can be seen in the old difficulty of the Patriarchs and the law of monogamous marriage, or the adulterous liason of Genesis 16. Issues such as these will cause little difficulty to the believer once a true appreciation of the process of God's revelation is achieved. This is all the more important, as instances such as these used to be adduced very often to illustrate the falsity of religious belief in those versions of popular agnosticism in the later nineteenth century and in those cultural backwaters where they still survive.

It is easy to note that these early images of God tended to see him merely in all-powerful terms, whereas the Hebrews were quick to grasp God's revelation of himself as just. This very early transition can be powerfully seen in the narratives relating to God's action in the Deluge incident, or in his destruction of Sodom and Gomorrah (Genesis 6—8; 18:19). These narratives are at pains to illustrate that Yahweh in these actions is not indulging in fickle and capricious anger, but that he is acting in a rational and a moral way. This was a concern which would have been quite out of place in the religious awareness of the authors of a document(s) such as the Epic of Gilgamesh. The pattern we can detect in the emergence of the Old Testament under God's inspiration is, in very general terms, a transition from a God of Power, to a God of Justice. The stages of development are only sketched in here for purposes of clarity in trying to discern a pattern within a short space of time. This process of transition in the giving of revelation reached its climax in the revelation of the God of Forgiveness, whose basic attribute is Love, in the New Testament. It is fatally easy to imagine a gulf between the Just images of God in the Old Testament and the Love images in the New. It is also easy to imagine the God of the New Testament to be motivated by some sort of mawkish and sentimental understanding of 'love'. The God of the Old Testament who was predominantly seen in terms of justice, and the God of the New seen predominantly in terms of love, are really quite close to each other. The just God of the Old Testament was also *hesed* and the God of love was most accurately described by *agape*, a word as inadequately rendered by 'love' now as it was when John and Paul wrote. Too often at present, especially in the tradition of the Jesus movements, Christian love and the God of love are trivialised in a way that suggests that this God has no standards. Christian forviveness is reduced to compromise and the Christian is forbidden to take any stand lest he offend against charity. These are travesties of the truth.

In very general terms you can note that the Hebrews in their grasp of revelation progressed from a God of Power to a God generally characterised by Justice, to a God of Love. As already noted these are rough divisions and they are certainly not mutually exclusive in the biblical tradition, but they do serve as useful indications. It is not so important to note the stages in the transition as to note the factors that caused the Hebrews to grasp those stages in God's revelation. Firstly we can note in that process that the Creator God is revealing himself according to the human capacity to receive. It is again fatally easy to construe this, as the Modernists did, as a revelation which is the product of human desire. A proper grasp of the way the Creator of a process will work in it will immediately disallow an understanding of revelation as some sort of human achievement. It is also worth noting that these three major images of God, justice, power and love, do not totally blend and harmonise with one another. They clash on the peripheries of what they assert, for, obviously, as we see these attributes, one cannot exercise unlimited and untrammeled power and still always act justly. What we see is that it was the assessed shortcomings in the Hebrew's earlier grasp of God's revelation that made them open to a deeper grasp of his nature in his revelation of himself as just. In short, it is the realisation of inadequacy in our knowledge of God revealing that opens us to the further grasp of his truth. In some forms of apologetics attempts used sometimes be made to face attacks by attempting to maintain that there were no difficulties with the faith. It was felt that to admit such would set in motion a process that would cause the whole edifice of the faith to collapse. In fact we clearly realise that there must always remain difficulties in the faith since its object is ultimately the infinite God whose nature can be authentically, but never exhaustively, grasped

57

within the bounds of human ideas and words. In this light it probably makes more sense to say that there are not difficulties with the faith itself, but with our grasp of it. It is the mystery of God that causes these inadequacies in our knowledge concerning him. Often we used be told: 'Don't ask questions, that's a mystery'. 'Mystery' seemed to be some sort of solid wall against which the mind came and after which all further efforts to understand were totally baffled. Albert Einstein, speaking of the object of physical science, also described it in terms of mystery, but by it he meant something that is so rich in meaning that the mind quickly breaks down in the effort to understand. This concept of mystery is of course eminently applicable to God the Revealer, and powerfully indicates the source of any difficulties we may encounter in this sphere.

IV. FAITH AS 'DISCERNMENT'

From a study of the process of God's Revelation to man several useful indications emerge. Firstly, we may expect God's interventions to be predominantly after the manner of the Creator, not creature. This may discourage an approach that can see the Divine Activity *only* in the extraordinary, inexplicable and dramatic. God after all is the author of this world, but we seem to have spent a great deal of the history of Christian reflection trying to banish him from what must be the most important sphere of his salvific activity. This is what we attempt when we *demand* that divine activity in the world has to be of the inexplicable and dramatic type: an interruption of the course of nature. Naturally we cannot legislate for God in saying what is possible for him to do and what is not, for our study of revelation's process indicates we grasp God's message to us in an inductive rather than in a predominantly deductive way. We cannot therefore on the very terms of the question know what is possible or impossible for God. It is clear that the giving of revelation was often accompanied by theophanies, but the ordinary mode of God's communication will still be through his creation in a suffused and hidden way which men of faith must discern. God's activity is hidden not because he tries to play a game with us or lead us on piecemeal, but because the activity of a creator in his creation will be a continual one. Anything that is ever-present or continual is never dramatic or noticeable: it may even be missed completely. Good examples are the air we breathe—we never notice it until it becomes scarce or uncomfortable, of the continual love of a mother for a child— again often not noticed until it is gone. God's presence in his creation is hidden for the sole reason that it is a creative presence and not one modeled on the type of presence appropriate to a creature. His presence and action must therefore be discerned by men of faith.

The terms we use to describe faith disclose our understanding of revelation. Where revelation is seen as a dramatic and completely unambiguous thing, faith will obviously be reduced to a passive recognition of this work of God. Where revelation is assessed as having no real existence in history it will be credited to faith as its invention. It is between these two extremes I would locate a true understanding of faith as 'discernment'. It implies that revelation can be hidden (for instance why did the crossing of the Red Sea not appear as revelatory in the same way to both Egyptians and Hebrews?) but at the same time really present. This avoids the extreme of maintaining a revelation of the interruptive, creaturely kind as the norm, and at the same time expresses that God really has and does intervene in this world. He reveals however in a way that places an *onus* on the observer in grasping its significance because of its essentially hidden nature. Faith as discernment then is to be understood as the mean between, on the one hand, a purely passive attitude where faith is reduced to recognition of the obvious, and on the other, an inventive exercise where there is really no objective revelation in history on which it may bear. The understandings of revelation that match these assessments of faith are obvious and I think this type of examination of the process by which God showed himself to men will provide us with an exceptionally useful paradigm for the way in which theological reflection on his revelation should be continued in a balanced way within the Church until the Second Coming when God's creative revealing process will have reached its goal.

Spirit

HOLY SPIRIT IN EARLY CHRISTIAN TEACHING

Thomas Marsh

The revival of theological interest in the Holy Spirit which has accompanied and been largely occasioned by the charismatic renewal movement has caught theology unawares. It is true that the documents of Vatican II display a deep interest in this theme and in the theological commentaries devoted to the Council one can point to some significant treatment of it. Nevertheless, because this has been for so long such a neglected theme in western theology, we are still only at the beginning of what one hopes will develop into a comprehensive pneumatology. In such situations theology's primary task is a positive one rather than a speculative or systematic one. The history of the doctrine needs to be written, and written rigidly in accordance with the canons of textual interpretation and historical method. The meaning of the elusive term 'Spirit' as it occurs in biblical and later theological texts needs to be precisely defined. The horizon of the concept in the various periods of its history needs to be drawn as tightly as possible. The shift of nuance from period to period needs to be marked. Only thus can the foundations be laid of a proper and permanent theology of the Spirit and only thus can a vague, arbitrary Spirit-theology be avoided.

In accordance with this programme this essay attempts to outline the history of the theology of the Spirit in early Christian teaching. Beginning with the New Testament itself, as represented by the two writers most interested in the theme, Luke and Paul, I will proceed to the developments which occur in this area in the following centuries. As with most New Testament themes, however, it is impossible to begin immediately with the New Testament documents themselves. For in this area above all the Old Testament background is essential to an understanding of New Testament thought and experience. I therefore wish to introduce the topic by a brief consideration of some aspects of this Old Testament background. The significance of this brief look at the Old Testament will, I hope, emerge in the course of the discussion.

Spirit of God in the Old Testament

The Old Testament concept of the Spirit of Yahweh begins as an interpretation of the charismatic activity which manifested itself in Israel at the time of the conquest and early settlement in the land of Canaan.[1] This extraordinary behaviour, surpassing the ordinary process of nature or the known ingenuity of man, was seen as an act of God and to safeguard the transcendence of God was attributed anthropomorphically to his ruah, his Spirit. Because this activity was abnormal, it was sudden, unexpected and transient. It represented a sudden, transient manifestation of God's power through his Spirit taking possession of and acting in certain persons. Those in whom this power appears are persons with public responsibility of one kind or another — warriors, leaders, prophets. Though it is the prophet who becomes especially associated with the Spirit in the mind of Isarel, it is important to remember that in fact the prophet is but one of the three categories of persons in whom the Spirit acts. From its origin in the experience of Israel the activity of the Spirit cannot therefore be confined to the concept of prophecy. It signifies broadly an act of power accomplished by God on behalf of his people. Even in the prophet it is not only the forceful communication of God's message which is attributable to the Spirit but also the extraordinary forms of activity which may accompany that communication. The power of the Spirit manifests itself in both word and work in warrior, leader and prophet. The expression 'prophetic Spirit' or 'Spirit of prophecy', which becomes the usual way of referring to the Spirit of God in late Judaism, is therefore on the one hand, as referring to the Spirit in the Old Testament economy, a form of synechdoche, one aspect of a phenomenon representing the whole, while at the same time it shows that by this period the Spirit had become exclusively identified with the prophetic experience.

It is necessary to stress the creative character of this early period in the history of Israel. It must be remembered that at this time Israel possessed no canonical scripture and no settled, consecrated body of tradition to structure and authenticate its faith. Where faith and its structures are concerned it is a period of creation The tradition which will later issue in scripture is in the process of formation. It is precisely this situation which calls forth and gives status and importance to the charismatic leader and the prophet. Where neither consecrated tradition nor canonical scripture can be appealed to, the prophet in particular becomes the recognised vehicle of revelation.

With the passage of time institutionalising forces encroached upon and came to absorb the charismatic elements in the life of Israel and even the theology of the Spirit which went with those elements.[2] The concept of the Spirit as a living reality was ultimately not able to survive this disappeareance of charismatic experience which had been its source. With the eventual acceptance by Israel of a canon of scripture the whole idea of continuing prophecy begins to appear superfluous and Judaism quite logically develops the doctrine of the quenched Spirit and the cessation of prophecy.[3] Prophecy and the Spirit of prophecy had served their purpose and belonged to the past.

Salvation history, however, still remained open-ended and Israel looked forward to the future and final saving act of God. In the prophets' presentation of this End-Time the Spirit of God is given a prominent place. The whole new community will be endowed with the prophetic Spirit.[4] The quenched Spirit will return. For late Judaism the Spirit is the prophetic Spirit.[5] The quenched Spirit who is awaited is the Spirit of prophecy.

The prophetic concept, however, is not the only concept of the Spirit in the Old Testament. There is another strand of thought, not very prominent but very significant for the future, which represents the Spirit as the creative and life-giving power of God. This concept is found in the creation accounts of Genesis and some other texts which look back to that *semel pro semper* act.[6] When the prophets come to describe the future age as a new creation they reintroduce this concept of the life-giving Spirit who will be the agent of this new creation and the source of its new life.[7] Late Judaism, however, does not appear to have paid much attention to this idea and it exerts little influence on its thought.

The New Testament

The writer who to my mind forms the best introduction to the New Testament theology of the Spirit is St Luke, and this for reasons which I hope will appear as we proceed. Though most of what will be said here will concern Acts, I wish to begin with a few observations on the Gospel. I would like to stress that Luke is perfectly consistent in the concept of the Spirit which he presents throughout both his works.[8]

THE PNEUMATOLOGY OF LUKE

a) The Gospel

A significant feature of Luke's portrayal of Jesus is his emphasis on his prophetic character. This emphasis begins with the first public appearance of Jesus which is at the baptism in the Jordan. This scene in all three Synoptics has a marked prophetic character. It is presented as in a sense the prophetic vocation of Jesus and his endowment with the prophetic Spirit.[9] This is the prophetic Spirit returning to Israel, the dawning of the new age. But Luke connects the subsequent ministry of Jesus more closely than Matthew or Mark with the illapse of the Spirit at the baptism by now bringing forward immediately Jesus' visit to Nazareth and giving us the comment on Isaiah 61:1-2. This passage is programmatic, an introductory statement of the significance of the ministry which it begins. In applying here this text to himself Jesus acknowledges his endowment with the prophetic Spirit of which the text speaks. The ministry which flows from this source is a prophetic ministry expressed in word and work, directed by the Spirit and informed with his *dynamis*.[10] Because this is the beginning of the new and final age, this gift of the Spirit in Jesus is the eschatological gift and therefore is not transient; it remains, it is permanent. It is not always active, but it is always there.

A significant feature of the concept of the Spirit here is that the Spirit is not a power at the disposal of Jesus, an agent he can put to work.[11] Rather Jesus is the agent directed by the Spirit and informed with his power. He is led by the Spirit (Lk 4:1). Also, in Jesus the gift of the Spirit does not take a charismatic form. Jesus is not a charismatic in any usual sense of that term.[12]

The Gospel thus shows us the primary emphases in Luke's theology of the Spirit. The Spirit here is the prophetic Spirit, the eschatological gift of God inaugurating the new age in his Son and Messiah, Jesus of Nazareth. As eschatological gift this presence of the Spirit is abiding and permanent, even if not always active. The activity of the Spirit in the ministry of Jesus is firmly in the prophetic tradition and consists of forceful preaching and works of power. The Spirit directs and empowers the ministry of Jesus. Charismatic phenomena are not part of this activity.

As we turn now to Acts of the Apostles we will find these same emphases reappearing there. The Spirit given to and abiding in the Church is a continuation and expansion of the Spirit-filled ministry of Jesus.

b) Acts of the Apostles

Luke opens his second volume, as he does the ministry of Jesus, with a programme note.[13] In the opening verses the Apostles, who represent the Church, are instructed by the risen Christ to wait in Jerusalem for the promise of the Father given through Jesus, the baptism of the Spirit.

Endowned with this gift and its power, the Church will go out to bear witness to Christ, from Jerusalem to Samaria, to the ends of the earth.

This note sets the scene for the story which follows: the gift of the Spirit of the Church and the successful mission guided, directed and empowered by the Spirit. It is the story of the Gospel all over again: the Spirit-directed, prophetic ministry of Jesus continues in the Spirit-directed, prophetic ministry of the Church.

The event of Pentecost is the true beginning of Acts. The description of this event in terms of wind and fire betokens an act of God. This is the community's endowment with the promised, eschatological gift of the Spirit. As eschatological this giving of the Spirit is full, final and permanent. It will not pass away or be withdrawn; it will ever remain the possession, or rather the endowment, of the community.

The nature and function of this gift of the Spirit to the Church is clearly indicated by Luke in his account of it: 'they were all filled with the Holy Spirit and began to speak in other tongues, as the Spirit gave them utterance' (2:4), i.e., the ability to convincingly preach the Gospel. This statement indicates where Luke wishes to put the emphasis. His Church is a missionary Church through its proclamation of the Gospel. Every aspect of its life is drawn into this task and becomes an expression of it. The whole life of the Church is a sermon. But the persuasive force of this sermon does not lie in human eloquence but in the power of the Spirit which from Pentecost on resides in the community and gives convincing force to its witness and preaching of its Lord. Luke's addition in v. 18 to the text of Joel is significant: '. . . and they shall prophesy. . .'. It is the prophetic Spirit who gives them utterance.

This ministry, like the ministry of Jesus himself, 'a prophet mighty in deed and word' (Lk 24:19), is likewise a prophetic ministry accomplished in word and work. It involves not only forceful preaching but also powerful and extraordinary deeds. The initiative always rests with the Spirit. The Spirit is not the instrument of the Church; the Church is the instrument of the Spirit. He it is who constantly guides, directs, strengthens and empowers the community and its missionary efforts.

The concept of the Spirit here, as in the Gospel, is that of the prophetic Spirit, the power of God acting in the words and works of men with a view to the forceful presentation of God's message.[14] As such the gift of the Spirit in Acts is not formally a sanctifying gift, it is not directly connected with the forgiveness of sins and it is not an effect of Baptism.[15] To assert otherwise would mean misconceiving the concept of the prophetic Spirit in biblical thought, misinterpreting particular texts of Acts and introducing a fundamental incoherence and inconsistency into the most coherent and consistent of all New Testament writers. The Spirit in Acts is the prophetic Spirit who enables the Church in manifold ways to proclaim the Gospel with power.

In so identifying Luke's concept of the Spirit, the question arises: What is the source of this concept and theology? Is it a construction of Luke himself or has he received it from his sources and if so can these sources be identified? Before one can answer these questions, one must first abstract from this theology of the Spirit those aspects which Luke himself has contributed to it. The most significant of these is the institutionalising tendency which his pneumatology presents. We know from the Pauline letters that charismatic activity was a feature of the life of the early Christian communities. One would not suspect this from the picture Luke gives of them.[16] His Church is a very rational Church as also is its preaching. Charismatic manifestations of the Spirit are exceptional and are almost totally confined to the initiation of significant missionary endeavours.[17] The ecstatic speech of Pentecost he interprets as a gift of foreign languages, a most useful missionary qualification.[18] He does mention prophets in the Church but he does not prominently feature them or give the impression that they are an important body or in any way specially endowed by the Spirit.[19] On the contrary, practically all the people in whom the Spirit is significantly at work in the developing mission are institutional figures and Church leaders, above all, Peter and Paul. Luke's Church is very definitely the Apostolic Church. The Spirit is given to all but he manifests himself especially in the office-holders. This institutionalising tendency is certainly Luke's own imposition on his material, though it is undoubtedly indicative also of the period and situation in which he is writing. We cannot therefore attribute this aspect of Luke's pneumatology to his sources nor can we use it to identify them.

The basic source from which this pneumatology ultimately derives can only be the early Jerusalem community itself. The reasons for this identification briefly are as follows:

1. It is a primitive, undeveloped pneumatology relative to that of Paul and therefore it is pre-Pauline.

2. It is thoroughly biblical and Jewish and without Hellenistic features.

3. It presents the concept of the Spirit predominant in late Judaism and thus would represent the thinking of the early community on the Spirit. — There is in fact no other way one could possibly imagine the early community thinking about the Spirit but as the Spirit of prophecy.

65

Basically, then, Luke's theology of the Spirit derives from the early Jerusalem community and presents us with the basic features of its pneumatology.[20] In this respect it presents a primitive pneumatology relative to other documents of the New Testament, the pneumatology in fact from which the others developed. We find here, therefore, the *terminus a quo* of New Testament theology of the Spirit. Luke has not essentially interfered with the concept of the Spirit which he had found in his sources. He does, however, play down the charismatic element in it and he presents the institutional leaders as the primary bearers of the Spirit.

THE PNEUMATOLOGY OF PAUL

The concept of the prophetic Spirit is also a familiar feature of Paul's pneumatology. The concept here again presents the basic features of the biblical tradition, viz., the power of God operating in word and work for the convincing preaching of the Gospel. 'Our gospel,' he writes in 1 Thess 1:5, 'came to you not only in word, but also in power and the Holy Spirit and with full conviction.' 'My speech and my message,' he states in 1 Cor 2:4-5, 'were not in plausible words of wisdom, but in demonstration of the Spirit and power, that your faith might not rest in the wisdom of men but in the power of God.' And in Rom 15:18-19 he speaks of 'what Christ has wrought through me... by word and work, by the power of signs and wonders, by the power of the Holy Spirit.' We have here the same concept and outlook as in Luke, the classic biblical concept of the prophetic Spirit and we may remark the familiarity of early Christianity with this concept and outlook.

Paul and Luke share the same key word for the operation of the Spirit, viz., *dynamis*. It would be wrong, I believe, to confine this term to miracles, to works, and not see it as also applying to preaching, to word. *Dynamis* refers to the activity of the Spirit in whatever form it manifests itself, in word or work. For the gospel is communicated in both these ways, or rather by a combination of both. And it is worth noting too that the Spirit is active not only in the preacher but also in the hearer. It is not the human preacher who convinces, converts and brings to faith, but the Holy Spirit whose power is at work in both preacher and hearer and leads the hearer to faith. The genesis of faith is the work of the Spirit.[21]

When one examines further this *dynamis* of the Spirit in Paul one sees that it includes prominently in its reference not only forceful preaching and miraculous activity but also a charismatic element.

Charismatic activity is here presented as a normal and prominent feature of Church life, even though not every Christian is by any means a charismatic in the extraordinary sense. This activity in all its many forms is a work of the prophetic Spirit, even though the role of the prophet in the Church, so prominently featured by Paul, refers to only one of these forms.

We see here basically the same concept of the Spirit as in Luke, though the charismatic element is more pronounced and this theology has therefore the same ultimate source as in Luke, the concept of the prophetic Spirit in the early community. But Paul, though he accepts the charismatic phenomena as a genuine operation of the Spirit, already reveals the institutionalising tendency at work which we have already noticed in a more advanced stage in Luke. The situation at Corinth clearly called for authoritative intervention and Paul's carefully thought-out analysis (1 Cor 12–13) marks the beginning of an institutionalising process which is going to have a long history. The basis of his approach and strategy lies, not only in his emphasis on the unity of source for the charism in the Spirit of God, but also on the community base of this source, i.e., the universality of the gift of the Spirit in the community. The Spirit is given to the community and is therefore shared in by all its members. From this it follows that it is not only those who display extraordinary phenomena who are truly charismatics, i.e., endowed with gifts by the Spirit; all Christians are charismatics because to each is given the manifestation of the Spirit (1 Cor 12:7). Official Church functions are thus placed among the charismata and finally the Christian life of *agape* is presented as the basic and finest charism and manifestation of the Spirit (1 Cor 13). Paul here plays down the value of the extraordinary phenomena by integrating pneumatology and ecclesiology, by interpreting the gift of the Spirit in terms of the community as body of Christ. He gives a theological justification and basis to the institutionalising tendency he here initiates.

Paul's concept of the Church as the body of Christ enables him to relate together the dynamic concept of the prophetic Spirit and his ecclesiology. Important though this contribution is, his major contribution to pneumatology, and therefore also ecclesiology, lies elsewhere. It was Paul who introduced into Christian thinking the concept of the *life-giving* Spirit. Here he was utterly original.[22] Ultimately, the future was to lie with this development and indeed but for it pneumatology could scarcely have survived in Christian theology or at least it could only survive in an attenuated form and as a minor theme.

I would like first to glance at the presence and scope of this concept in Paul and then at his source for the concept and the process of thought whereby he evolved it.

The texts which most explicitly present this concept are Romans 8:2, 1 Corinthians 15:45 and 2 Corinthians 3:6, though once one has recognised it one can see it in many other texts too. Contrasting Christian existence with existence under the law, Paul in Romans 8:2 describes the former as 'the law of the Spirit of life in Christ Jesus'. In 1 Corinthians 15:45 he states: 'the last Adam (= Christ) became a life-giving Spirit'. In 2 Corinthians 3:6 he states plainly: 'The Spirit gives life'.

Paul presents Christian existence as a life, new life in Christ. The principle of this new life is the Spirit who is thus introduced as the Spirit of life, the life-giving Spirit. Once this concept is recognised, the influence which it exerts on Paul's thought on Christian existence and life is easy to recognise. Christian existence means new life in the Spirit which expresses itself in the fruits of the Spirit (Gal 5:16-26). From this pneumatology Paul quite logically derives his supreme moral principle: 'If we live by the Spirit, let us also walk by the Spirit' (Gal 5:25; cf. Rom 8:4, 14; Gal 5:16, 18).

What is the source of this concept in Paul? No doubt many strands influence Paul's thinking on the Spirit and much has been made of Hellenistic ideas of pneuma as shaping his pneumatology. But Paul's thought ever remains firmly rooted in the Bible and Jewish thinking and the influence of Hellenistic concepts can only too easily be exaggerated. In 2 Corinthians 3:2-3 he himself has indicated, I think, his chief source for this concept of the Spirit: 'You yourselves are our letter of recommendation, written on your hearts, to be known and heard by all men; and you show that you are a letter from Christ delivered by us, written not with ink but with the Spirit of the living God, not on tablets of stone but on tablets of human hearts.' This text sends us directly to Ezekiel 36:26-27 (and Jeremiah 31:31-33), with which one must also associate Ezekiel 37, the vision of the dry bones which depicts the new creation and where in v. 14 God tells the prophet: 'I will put my Spirit within you and you shall live,' a verse given a Christian application here in 2 Corinthians 3:6. The prophets' presentation of the messianic age as the new creation is Paul's source for his concept of the life-giving Spirit. The process of thought whereby he developed his idea would seem to have run along the following lines. The prophets depict the messianic age as a time of renewal of land and people, a renewal which Isaiah 65: 17; 67:22, explicitly term a new creation. Paul identifies the risen Christ and the redemption he represents as the fulfilment of this prophecy, as the new creation, Col 1:15-20, 2 Cor 5:17, Gal 6:15. But the prophets in this context had reintroduced the life-giving Spirit of the first creation as again the new life-giving principle of the new messianic creation. That Paul follows them in their sweep of thought is clear from 1 Corinthians 15:45.[23] The Old Testament text in question here is Genesis 2:7, which Paul develops christologically, as also does John 20: 22. Paul is now able to quickly and easily integrate the christology and the pneumatology. The power of God raising Jesus to life and in him sharing this new life with men is the Spirit and so the Spirit poured out on the Church is the life-giving Spirit, the agent of the new creation and the source of its life. Christology and pneumatology thus integrated together then issue in an appropriate ecclesiology and theology of grace and Christian living. We are here, I believe, at the heart of the Pauline theological synthesis.

Central to this theology is the close relationship almost but never quite to the point of identification between Christ and the Spirit.[24] The Spirit in Paul is the Spirit of Christ and becomes in Christians 'the Spirit of life in Christ Jesus' (Rom 8:2). Paul's pneumatology contrasts sharply here with Luke's who does not relate Christology and pneumatology as closely or explicitly as this and for whom Christ and the Spirit, though certainly related, remain nevertheless more independent figures;[25] Here again Luke's pneumatology shows itself more primitive and less developed than the Pauline.

This new development in pneumatology by Paul is loaded with theological implications, though one should not imagine that Paul was aware of these. One should note in particular how it links the Spirit very intimately with the ministry of the Church, especially its sacramental ministry, since it is through this ministry that the Spirit operates his life-giving function.[26]

We are now in a position to summarily compare the pneumatologies of Paul and Luke.

1. *Concept of the Spirit*
   This is consistently prophetic in Luke, prophetic and life-giving in Paul; Luke's is the more primitive concept. Paul's the more developed.

2. *Source*
   The early Christian community is the source of the concept of the prophetic Spirit in both Paul and Luke; the concept of the life-giving Spirit is Paul's own original development.

3. *Charismatic Activity*
   This is more prominent in Paul and more central in his pneumatology; this reflects his earlier period.

4. *Institutionalising Tendency*
   This is beginning already in Paul but is still more developed in Luke; prophecy is more institutional in Luke. This again reflects Luke's later period.

5. *Relation of Christ and the Spirit*

They are closely linked in Paul, more distinct in Luke. Here again Paul's is the more developed theology and Luke's the more primitive.

Paul's theology of the Spirit, therefore, is much more developed than Luke's which is more primitive in comparison. This should warn us not to take Paul's thought as the general level of Christian thinking in the first century. Luke, though later, is theologically both more primitive and more representative, as second century Christian literature will bear out.

EARLY CHRISTIAN LITERATURE

The non-canonical Christian literature of the first and early second centuries displays an outlook very similar to that of the later documents of the New Testament. This is a literature as yet little influenced by the New Testament writings and it pre-dates the formation of the Canon. It is a continuation of the New Testament rather than a reflection upon it. In the area of pneumatology the striking feature is the infrequency of reference to the Spirit and the insignificance of most of the references which do occur.[27] The Spirit here is a very minor theme, a feature which this literature shares with most of the later New Testament documents.[28]

The Spirit is consistently understood in these early Christian writings as the prophetic Spirit.[29] He is above all the inspirer of the Old Testament scripture treated generally as prophecy fulfilled in Christ. Of the Pauline theology of the Spirit of life there is no trace whatever. Indeed, Pauline thought generally is conspicuous by its absence in these documents.[30] One does find, however, an insistence on the eschatological gift of the Spirit to the Church and his abiding presence in it and its members. But this insistence only further emphasises the absence of a significant Spirit theology.

The reason for this absence of a vital pneumatology lies in the gradual decline of the charismatic element in the Church and of the office of the prophets.[31] It was this experiential context which called forth the theology of the prophetic Spirit and made it a living theology. But as this experience fades so also does this theology, while the Pauline development has not apparently taken sufficient root to fill the vacuum. *Pari passu* with this disappearance of charismatic and prophetic features in the Church there goes the growth and development of institutional elements. There is a strong emphasis on sound doctrine and Church structures and authority while later in the second century there comes the development of the New Testament Canon. It is noteworthy, however, that the theological justification claimed for authority and its structures does not include any appeal to the presence of the Spirit, apart from the concept of scriptural inspiration. It would, however, be a serious misinterpretation of these developments to see them as a simple case of Institution versus Charism.[32] Rather these institutional developments were themselves seen as charism but significant reference to the Spirit does not enter into theology. This was an ecclesiology without the Spirit. The inadequacy of this position will be felt later in the second century and a significant aspect of the revival of pneumatology then will consist in furnishing this ecclesiology with its necessary pneumatological basis.

A further influential factor in the disappearance of the theology of the Spirit is to be found in the outlook of Judaeo-Christianity. For it too is characterised by an almost total neglect of the Spirit. This may be summarily illustrated by the way John 3:5 is treated in the *Recognitions of Clement*. In *Recognitions* 6:9, this text is in effect quoted twice: 'Unless a man is born of water, he shall not enter the kingdom of heaven,' and again: 'When you are regenerated and born again of water and of God...'[33] The suppression of the reference to the Spirit, on which the whole point of Christ's statement in John hinges, is quite deliberate and is typical of this literature.[34] The reason for this antipathy to the Spirit on the part of Judaeo-Christianity lies in the anti-Pauline polemic which is one of its main preoccupations. Paul opposed the Spirit to the Law. In reasserting the Law against Paul, Judaeo-Christianity has to combat Paul's theology of the Spirit and this it does by ignoring it.

It is against this experiential and theological background that one must understand the undeveloped state of the third article of the early Creed: 'I believe in the Holy Spirit.'[35] The bare reference to the Spirit in the developing Creeds of the second century is startling evidence of the low Spirit-theology of this period. Indeed, the development of the Creed itself and its kindred formula, the *regula fidei*, the appeal to an authoritative tradition and the formation of the early New Testament Canon were all inimical to the concept of the charismatic, prophetic Spirit active in the Church. The coup-de-grace was finally delivered in the strong reaction of the Church to the re-appearance of a prophetic order in Montanism. This proved the death-blow for the admittedly diminishing charismatic element in the Church and its theology of the prophetic Spirit, though it is both interesting and important to note that the principle or theory of the Spirit's charismatic presence was not questioned.[36] But the practice was now definitely suspect and the remnants of it left gradually and quietly disappear. Thus deprived of its experiential base the already frail theology of the prophetic Spirit inevitably expired also.

At this stage it will be useful to pause and consider the peculiar but logical similarity which now emerges between the Old Testament experience of the prophetic Spirit and the Christian.

The Old Testament theology of the Spirit begins at an early formative stage of the religion of Israel and it is rooted in charismatic experience. The theological interpretation which grows out of this experience is gradually subected to rationalising and institutionalising influences which finally result in the almost total disappearance of the charismatic element and the appeal to the Spirit which it involved. The theology of the quenched Spirit was the logical outcome.

The theology of the Spirit in early Christianity follows a similar pattern. This theology grows out of charismatic experience as its interpretation and it is expressed in terms of the biblical and Jewish concept of the prophetic Spirit. Gradually the charismatic experience fades and the rational, institutionalising elements develop. The result once again is that the theology of the Spirit, now deprived of its experiential base, fades also.

THE REVIVAL OF PNEUMATOLOGY

Christianity was prevented from arriving at any concept of a quenched Spirit through its belief in the eschatological character of the gift of the Spirit. The Spirit is an abiding gift leading to eternal life. Granted this belief it could only be a matter of time until study of the New Testament would lead to an appreciation of the Pauline and Johannine pneumatology and therefore to a rediscovery of the theology of the Spirit as interpreting, not simply a particular aspect of Christian life such as the charismatic, but the very essence of the Church and Christian existence. This discovery or re-discovery begins in the latter part of the second century and the man responsible for it was Irenaeus.

The occasion which led to this new development was, I believe, the threat of Gnosticism. The Gnostic sects seem to have cashed in on the Church's neglect of the Spirit and to have attempted to appropriate the Spirit to themselves.[37] This was especially true of the Valentinians. Condemning Church baptism with faint praise they made great play of the gift of the Spirit which they themselves claimed to confer in their post-baptismal rite of anointing.[38] Here only was the Spirit given and only those who had so received the Gnostic gift of the Spirit were true Christians and entitled to the name of Christian and possessed the

72

assurance of salvation. Saying 95 of *The Gospel of Philip* states this position quite clearly:

> The chrism is superior to baptism, for from the chrism are we called Christians, not because of the baptism; and Christ is (so) called because of the chrism. For the Father anointed the Son, and the Son anointed the apostles, and the apostles anointed us. He who is anointed possesses the All. He possesses the resurrection, the light, the Cross, the Holy Spirit.[39]

This is the context which explains the statement of the Valentinian Theodotus: 'Many are the hylic, not many are the psychic, but few and far between are the pneumatic,' where the hylic refers to pagans, the psychic are orthodox Christians who have received Church baptism and the pneumatics are the Gnostics who have received the Spirit in the Gnostic initiation rite of anointing.[40]

This position refused to the Church the power to bestow the Spirit and denied it the possession of the Spirit. Thus, at the very moment that its theology of the Spirit had reached perhaps its lowest ebb, the Church's very existence was challenged precisely on this ground. This was a challenge it clearly could not ignore. It responded with vehemence in the writings especially of Irenaeus, Clement of Alexandria, Tertullian, Hippolytus. Irenaeus was here the first to really discover again and assert the Pauline and Johannine theology of the life-giving Spirit who gives existence and life to the Church and the Christian.[41] The sacramental source of Christian life gets particular emphasis. It is now that the epiclesis of the Spirit begins to make its appearance in the liturgy of the sacraments and that sacramental effects begin to be attributed to the agency of the Spirit.[42] Christian life in the individual and the community now again begins to be described as life in the Spirit. So Irenaeus can say: 'Where the Church is, there is the Spirit of God, and where the Spirit of God is, there is the Church and every kind of grace' (*Adv. Haer.* 4, 33, 9). Augustine's concept of the Spirit as the soul of the Church is here already in embryo.

This rediscovery through the Pauline theology of the dimension of the Spirit in the Church does not challenge the Church's institutional structure. Rather it gives it its necessary pneumatological basis. This theology, therefore, now takes firm root in the Church's consciousness and it is not destined to disappear. The denial of the divinity of the Spirit entailed in the Arian heresy gives this developing pneumatology a further fillip just when the great Pauline exegetes such as John Chrysostom are at hand to explain the New Testament texts. It is precisely the life-giving function of the Spirit which provides the orthodox with their answer to the Macedonian heresy. For if the Spirit gives divine life, he must be truly divine. Arius himself had ignored the question of the Spirit's divinity and it was not an issue at Nicaea. Hence, the creed of Nicaea in its third article had contented itself with simply repeated the old, traditional and bare creedal formula: 'We believe in the Holy Spirit'.[43] By the time of Constantinople in 381, however, the divinity of the Spirit had become a burning issue and the old formula was now clearly insufficient as a statement of orthodox faith. The nude third article of Nicaea is therefore now considerably expanded in the reworking of this creed at Constantinople:

> We believe in the Holy Spirit, the Lord and *giver of life (to zoo-poion),* who proceeds from the Father, who with the Father and the Son is together worshipped and together glorified, *who spoke through the prophets.*[44] (Italics inserted).

The reference to the Spirit 'who spoke through the prophets' repeats an old anti-Marcion formula going back to the second century and recalls the theology of the prophetic Spirit of that era.[45] But the description of the Spirit as 'life-giving' marks the importance of this concept in the fourth century and indicates the Pauline basis of the pneumatology then current.[46]

AFTERMATH

The controversial Spirit-theology of the fourth century incurred the danger of confining pneumatology within the area of the immanent Trinity, to questions of procession and relation, and of ignoring the economic Trinity, the role of the Spirit in the history of salvation and in the experience of the Church. By and large Greek theology succeeded in avoiding this danger and developed a living theology of the Spirit giving a prominent pneumatological dimension to its ecclesiology. Western theology, on the other hand, largely succumbed to the danger, mainly through the greater emphasis which it gave to Augustine's doctrine of appropriation. Applying this concept strictly meant seeing the Spirit as such operative only within the Trinity and the life of the Church was thus removed from his personal influence. To speak of the Spirit in the Church could only be a manner of speaking. As Augustine's pneumatology was the most comprehensive of the whole patristic period, especially in dynamically relating the themes of Spirit and Church, it was ironical that he should here unwittingly take with the left hand what he had so generously given with the right. The concentration of western ecclesiology on visible Church structures also kept the theology of Spirit and Church separate and distinct and helped further to confine pneumatology to the rarified sphere of the immanent Trinity. It is surely significant that in his magisterial treatment of Prophecy in the Summa (II-II, 171-174), as sensitive a listener to tradition as Aquinas has no significant reference to the Spirit of God.

The theology of the Spirit in the West thus tended to remain abstract, theoretic and remote from life. It is only when in our own times ecclesiology begins to expand that a new revival of pneumatology begins to take place. The importance of this theme in the documents of Vatican II is both a sign of that revival and a call for its development.

NOTES

1. For general studies of the Spirit of God in the Old Testament, cf. D. Lys, *'Ruach', Le Souffle dans l'Ancien Testament* (Paris 1962); G. T. Montague, *The Holy Spirit: Growth of a Biblical Tradition* (New York 1976); W. Eichrodt, *Theology of the Old Testament*, II, E.T. (London, 1967).
2. Examples of this institutionalising of the gift of the Spirit may be seen in the references to the gift as *permanent* (e.g. 1 Sam 16:13) and *transmissible* (e.g. Deut 34:9).
3. *Tosefta Sotah* 13, 2: 'When the last prophets, Haggai, Zechariah and Malachi died, the Holy Spirit ceased out of Israel', Strack-Billerbeck, *Kommentar zum Neuen Testament ans Talmud und Midrasch,* I (Munich 1922) 127. Cf. W. Forster, *Palestinian Judaism in New Testament Times,* E.T. (London 1964) 4-5.
4. Joel 3:1; Is 59:21. Moses' wish, Num 11:29, was an influential text here, cf. Strack-Billerbeck, op. cit. II (Munich 1924) 129-134.
5. Cf. Strack-Billerbeck, op. cit. II, 127-128. The Palestinian Targums regularly translate the biblical expressions 'the Spirit of Yahweh', 'the Spirit of God', etc. by 'the Spirit of prophecy'. Thus, e.g. Is 61: 1, 'The Spirit of the Lord God is upon me. . . ' becomes 'The Spirit of prophecy from before the Lord is upon me. . .' Cf. G. F. Moore, *Judaism in the First Centuries of the Christian Era,* I (Cambridge, Mass., 1927) 237, 421; M. McNamara, *Targum and Testament — Aramaic Paraphrases of the Hebrew Bible: A Light on the New Testament* (Shannon 1972) 113.
6. Gen 1:2 (a problematic text but cf. Lys, op. cit., 176ff; Montague, op. cit., 64ff), 2:7; Ps 33:6? Job 26:13; 33:4; Judith 16:14. Cf. P. van Imschoot, 'L'Esprit de Jahve, Source de vie dans l'Ancien Testament', in *Revue Biblique* 44 (1935) 481-501.
7. Ez 36:26-27; 37:14; Is 32:15-19; 44:3-4.
8. There is one exception, Luke 1:35, but this, significantly, belongs to the special infancy material.
9. This is not to suggest that the Synoptic account of the baptism sees the concept of prophet as an adequate description of Jesus and his ministry. This is not so, as the reference to sonship shows, Mt 3:17,

Mk 1:11, Lk 3:22. But it is here, as elsewhere, an important christo-logical model and particularly so in Luke. Cf. I. de la Potterie, 'L'Onction du Christ', in *Nouvelle Revue Theologique* 80 (1958) 225-52; F. Lentzen-Deis, *Die Taufe Jesu nach den Synoptikern* (Frankfurt-am-Main 1970) 270ff.

10. Cf. I. de la Potterie, art. cit.

11. Cf. J. E. Yates, 'Luke's Pneumatology and Luke 11:20' in *Studia Evangelica* II (Berlin 1964) 295-98. This point is significant for the argument concerning the original text of the important logion Mt 12:28 (Spirit of God) = Lk 11:20 (finger of God). It shows that Luke could quite easily have suppressed a reference to the Spirit in the tradition which he found conflicting with his own concept.

12. *Pace* J. D. G. Dunn, *Jesus and the Spirit* (London 1975) 87-88: 'He (Jesus) was charismatic in the sense that he manifested a *power* and *authority* which was not his own, which he neither achieved nor con-jured up, but which was given him, his by virtue of the Spirit/power of God upon him' (Italics original). While this statement gives a good Pauline theological definition of charismatic—ordinary usage is much looser—not even Paul, not to mention the other New Testament writers, applies the term to Jesus Christ or even suggests the legiti-macy of such application. This fact must be significant. Cf. J. Jere-mias, *New Testament Theology I: The Proclamation of Jesus.* E.T. (London 1971) 79-80.

13. On the pneumatology of Acts, cf. E. Trocme, 'Le Saint-Esprit et l'Eglise d'apres le livre des Actes', in *L'Esprit Saint et l'Eglise* (Paris 1969) 19-27; J. McPolin, 'The Holy Spirit in the Lucan and the Johannine Writings', in *Irish Theological Quarterly* 45 (1978) 117-31.

14. Cf. I. de la Potterie, art. cit.

15. Cf. T. Marsh, 'A Study of Confirmation I', in *Irish Theological Quar-terly* 39 (1972) 149-63. Note Acts 5:32: '. . . the Holy Spirit whom God has given to those who obey him'. The Spirit here is not the cause or principle of righteousness but the reward or gift of God to those who have already achieved righteousness. This notion of the gift of the Spirit as God's crowning reward to the just man is pro-minent in the wisdom literature and late Judaism. But the Spirit here firmly remains the prophetic Spirit.

16. Notice the absence of charismatic features in the summaries, Acts 2: 42-47; 4:32-35; 5:12-16.

17. E.g. Acts 2:1-4 (Pentecost); 8:14-17 (Samaria mission); 10:44-48 (Cornelius, the Gentile mission); 13:1-4 (Paul's mission); 19:1-6 (Ephesus mission). 4:31 is the exception.

18. Acts 2:4-13.

19. Cf. E. Earle Ellis, 'The Role of the Christian Prophet in Acts', in *Apostolic History and the Gospel, Biblical and Historical Essays presented to F. F. Bruce*, ed. W. Ward Gasque and Ralph P. Martin (Exeter 1970) 55-67: 'Although prophecy is a possibility for any Christian, it is primarily identified with certain leaders who exercise it as a ministry', 56. Note, for example, how Judas and Silas, called 'prophets' in 15:32, are described as 'leading men of the brother-hood' in 15:22.

20. One can, therefore, make the same claim for the pneumatology of Acts as S. S. Smalley makes for its christology when he describes it as 'essentially primitive in character', 'The Christology of Acts Again', in *Christ and Spirit in the New Testament: Studies in honour of C F. D. Moule,* ed. B. Lindars and S. S. Smalley (Cambridge 1973) 92.

21. Cf. P. Grech, 2 Cor 3:17 and the Pauline Doctrine of Conversion', in *Catholic Biblical Quarterly* 17 (1951) 420-37; I. de la Potterie, L'Onction du Chretien par la Foi', in I. de la Potterie and S. Lyonnet, *La Vie Selon l'Esprit* (Paris 1965) 107-168 (originally *Biblica* 40 [1959] 12-69).

22. Clearly there is no way of *proving* that Paul was actually the first to develop and apply this concept. But in the historical context the idea was original and only a bold penetrating mind .in a flash of insight would hit on it. Since it first occurs in Paul and since his mind was clearly of this kind, it seems a reasonable assumpiton that he was the first to conceive it.

23. Cf. J. D. G. Dunn, 'I Corinthians 15:45—Last Adam, life-giving Spirit', in *Christ and Spirit in the New Testament,* ed. Lindars and Smalley, 127-41. C. K. Barrett, commenting on this text in his *The First Epistle to the Corinthians* (London 1971²) 374, writes: 'Spirit is (for Paul, as in biblical thought generally) not merely alive but creatively life-giving'. This is an example of the common tendency to ignore the distinction between the prophetic and life-giving concepts of the Spirit. Once this distinction is blurred the history of pneumatology, both in Judaism and Christianity, becomes impossible to understand. If in biblical thought the Spirit was conceived as *essentially* life-giving, Judaism could never have arrived at its concept of the quenched Spirit.

24. Cf. J. D. G. Dunn, art. cit.; id., *Jesus and the Spirit,* 318-325.

25. Cf. H. Flender, *St Luke: Theologian of Redemptive History*, E.T. (London 1967) 135ff.

26. The concept of the life-giving Spirit is also a Johannine theme, e.g. John 3:5-6, 8; 6:63; 20:22-23 and the association in this Gospel of (life-giving) water and the Spirit. Cf. J. McPolin, art. cit.

27. The theology of the Spirit in the second century has been little studied. The following are useful: H. G. Swete, *The Holy Spirit in the Ancient Church* (London 1912). G. L. Prestige, *God in Patristic Thought* (London 1952²); A. Benoit, *Le Baptême Chrétien au Second Siècle* (Paris 1953); J. Daniélou, *The Development of Christian Doctrine before the Council of Nicaea, I: The Theology of Jewish Christianity*, E.T. (London 1964).

28. E. Trocme, art. cit. 19-21, points out that of 60 references to the Holy Spirit in Acts, 40 occur in chapters 1-11 and 20 in chapters 12—28. These figures would seem to be significant and would appear to be related to the diminishing interest in the theme of the Spirit on the part of most of the later documents of the New Testament.

29. It is sometimes thought that the references in the *Pastor of Hermas* to unethical conduct 'grieving the Spirit', e.g. Mand. 10, *passim*, indicates a concept of the Spirit as the principle of Christian ethical life. This is not so. This is the thoroughly Jewish concept of God's gift of the prophetic Spirit as the crowning reward of the just man; cf. *supra* n. 15.

30. A. Benoit, op. cit., p.228: 'Les concéptions pauliniennes proprement dites sont totalement étrangères à la pensée des Pères du second siècle'. Irenaeus, however, has to be made an exception here, as Benoit, whose reference is mainly to baptismal theology, concedes, though not sufficiently I think, 186ff.

31. A simple comparison of 1 Cor 12, *Didache* 11 and *Pastor of Hermas,* Mand. 11 is revealing for the decline of the prophetic office. Cf. James J. Ash, Jnr., 'The Decline of Ecstatic Prophecy in the Early Church' in *Theol. Studies* 37 (1976) 227-52; J. D. G. Dunn, *Jesus...,* 345ff.

32. Cf. James J. Ash, Jnr, art. cit. Ash's contention that the early *episcopos* did not oust the office of prophet but subsumed it, is, I think, correct—it can be supported by significant texts in early Christian literature—and supports the point made here that the decline of charismatic elements and the parallel growth of institutional elements in the early Church should not be read in simplistic terms as a survival of the fittest between institution and charism.

33. The extant text of the *Recognitions of Clement* is a fourth century document based on a second century source. The suppression of the reference to the Spirit here clearly comes from the second century original, since it reflects the context of Judaeo-Christian thought of that era. It would be impossible in the fourth century.

34. Elchasaite baptism was administered in the name of God and the Son, with no reference to the Spirit, cf. Hippolytus, *Philosoph.* 9, 10.

35. Cf. J. N. D. Kelly, *Early Christian Creeds* (London 1972³): the old (second century) Roman Creed, 152-5, other early western and eastern creeds, 172-6.

36. Cf. J. L. Ash, Jnr, art cit. Note, e.g., the statement in the anti-Montanist document written by an eastern bishop probably in the 180s A.D. and quoted by Eusebius, *Hist. Eccles.* 5, 17: 'For the prophetic gift must continue in the whole Church until the final coming.'

37. Gnosticism, it must be remembered, was never a unity and the Gnostic doctrine of the Spirit varied greatly. Cf. R. McL. Wilson, 'The Spirit in Gnostic Literature', in *Christ and Spirit in the New Testament,* ed. Lindars and Smalley, 345-58. The sects of Valentinus and Marcion were perhaps closest to the orthodox Church both in theology and liturgical practice.

38. Cf. A. Orbe, 'Teología Bautismal de Clemente Alejandrino', in *Gregorianum* 36 (1955) 410-48; W. C. van Unnick, 'The Ideas of the Gnostics concerning the Church,' in *The Birth of the Church*, E.T. (New York 1968) 225-42.

39. R. McL. Wilson, *The Gospel of Philip* (London 1962) 50.

40. *Extracts from Theodotus* 56 (ed. F. Sagnard, *Clement d'Alexandre: Extraits de Theodote*, SC23, Paris 1948).

41. H. G. Swete, op. cit. 89: 'Irenaeus enters into the details of the Holy Spirit's work on the hearts and lives of men with a fullness which is far in advance of other Christian writers of the second century.' Cf. J. Danielou, op. cit. 362-64.

42. Cf. T. Marsh, 'A Study of Confirmation III', in *Irish Theological Quarterly* 40 (1973) 125-147.

43. Denzinger 125. Cf. J. N. D. Kelly, op. cit. 152-55.

44. Denzinger 150. Cf. J. N. D. Kelly, op. cit. 338-44.

45. Novatian, *De Trinitate* 29, is typical: '*unus ergo et idem Spiritus qui in prophetis et apostolis.*' Cf. A. Orbe, *La Unción de Verbo* (Rome 1961) 53ff.

46. Cf. J. N. D. Kelly, loc. cit.

DISCERNMENT OF SPIRITS – A NEGLECTED GIFT

James D. G. Dunn

There are not very many points of contact between modern radical New Testament scholarship and the Pentecostal Movement. But there are *two* rather striking similarities: both recognise the importance of *prophecy* in first century Christianity, and both have *failed* to appreciate what was involved in first century Christian prophecy. Thus, on the one hand, Bultman strongly affirms the role of early Christian prophets in shaping the traditions about Jesus. The churches, he believes, ascribed the utterances of such prophets to be ascended Christ and made *no* distinction between sayings of the ascended Jesus and sayings spoken by Jesus during his earthly ministry—they were *all* sayings of Jesus and authoritative as such.[1] Consequently we have all the modern difficulty of ascertaining whether any particular saying goes back to Jesus as such or really derives originally from tha later context of the early Christian (prophetic) communities. Similarly E. Kasemann affirms with equal conviction that

> countless 'I' sayings of the Christ who revealed himself through the mouth of prophets gained entry into the Synoptic tradition as sayings of Jesus.[2]

But did the first Christians accept so readily everything that was said by a prophet or one who spoke under inspiration? Did they automatically assume that every inspired utterance was a word of the exalted Christ? I think not. Bultmann and Kasemann have neglected the important role filled by the 'gift of discernment'.

On the other hand Pentecostals and Pentecostal literature have also made much of first century Christian inspired utterance. Glossolalia has usually filled the centre of the stage, whether Pentecostals wished it so or not. But they have generally taken to heart the fact that Paul valued prophesy more highly than glossolalia (in the assembly at least) and will generally attempt to give it greater prominence in communal worship. One of the things which excites Pentecostals and charismatics so much is the sense that they are experiencing just what the first Christians experienced—the thrill of the prophetic Spirit restored to God's people when it seemed to have been withdrawn for so long, the wonder that God should be speaking so directly to his people once more. But, unfortunately, Pentecostals too have failed to appreciate the importance of the 'gift of discernment'. Where Paul links prophecy and discernment very closely, the typical Pentecostal exposition of the gifts of the Spirit in I Cor 12:8-10 has separated them, with prophecy treated as a gift of speech, and discernment linked usually to exorcism—a discerning of (evil) spirits to be 'cast out'.

Now I wish very much to emphasise the importance of first century Christian prophecy too. It is evident from the Synoptics that Jesus experienced the Spirit very largely as the Spirit of prophecy; evident too that the first Christians understood their own experience from Pentecost onwards very much in terms of the eschatological Spirit of prophecy. Moses' ancient hope that *all* God's people should be prophets (Num 11:29) had been fulfilled; Joel's prediction for the last days had been fulfilled—their sons and daughters, young and old, manservant and maidservant were all being inspired to prophesy (Acts 2:17ff). The Spirit was very much an immediate *fact* of their experience—not some dogman, or traditional belief, but a power that transformed lives, inspired speech, wrough miracles.[3] So too I believe that not a few prophetic utterances were recognised as words of the exalted Jesus; and no doubt in a number of instances these were grouped with other sayings of Jesus and then set down as such, to be included in due course in the Synoptic Gospels. The best example of this, I always think, is Mt 18:20.

However, it is the *other* side of the coin I wish to examine in this paper. For if the first Christians recognised that the prophetic Spirit had been restored, they recognised too the danger of *false* prophecy. Contrary to Bultman and the more radical form-critics, we can *not* assume that the first Christians simply accepted every inspired utterance as a saying of the exalted Christ. The first Christians were not slow to recognise that there were other possible sources of inspiration, that inspiration was not after all self-authenticating, that every prophecy had to be tested, weighed, assessed before it could be approved as a word of God. It is this neglected 'gift of discernment' that I want to study more closely.

1. *The importance of the gift of discernment within the biblical and early Christian tradition.*

Throughout the most vigorous period of Israelite prophecy the problem of false prophecy continually crops up and is never finally resolved. It first emerges in various episodes from the period of the judges and the early monarchy—Abimelech and the men of Shechem, Saul and his black moods, David and the numbering of Israel (Judg 9:23; 1 Sam 16: 14; 18:10f; 19:9f; 2 Sam 24:1-17). In each case actions of the charismatic leader of the time are attributed to inspiration from Yahweh, even though they were manifestly evil or in the event judged to be mistaken. These passages highlight *the ambiguity of inspiration*, whether it be of word or deed. And thereafter the awareness of this ambiguity, the sense of the ever-present danger of false prophecy, even in the mouth of a sincere and honourable prophet haunts the pages of the Old Testament. Classic expressions of this problem are 1 Kings 13 and 22, and Jeremiah. In 1 Kings 13 two prophets claim to exercise genuine prophetic ministry but speak conflicting oracles, and the 'false prophet' speaks both lies and a true word from Yahweh, whereas it is the 'true prophet' who is led astray and brought to judgment. In 1 Kings 22 the famous encounter between Ahab and the prophet Micaiah is described, with Micaiah denouncing the contrary military advice from the four hundred prophets as the product of a lying spirit put in their mouth by Yahweh. And in Jeremiah, that so honest prophet, we see coming to expression the self-questioning and doubt which must rack any prophet whose inspired utterances are pessimistic and unpopular—particularly 15:18b and 20:7.

Whilt thou be to me like a deceitful brook, like waters that fail?

O Lord thou hast deceived me, and I was deceived;
    thou art strongr than I, and thou has prevailed.
I have become a laughing stock all the day;
    everyone mocks me.

In these words the confident claim and counter-claim of competing prophets is left far behind, and the problem of false prophecy achieves its most anguished expression, where even the consciousness of overwhelming inspiration (20:9) gives the prophet himself no assurance that his words are true.

Turning to the New Testament period it becomes quickly evident that the early Christian churches were equally well aware of the danger of false prophecy. Thus Mt 7:15ff—'Beware of false prophets, who come to you in sheep's-clothing but inwardly are ravening wolves'. In addition Mark and Matthew have Jesus warning against the danger of false prophets (Mk 13:22/Mt 24:24; Mt 24:11), and Luke attributes a saying to Jesus which warns disciples against seeking a popularity like that enjoyed by the false prophets of old (Lk 6:26). According to Luke, moreover, the first major outreach from Jerusalem soon encountered the false inspiration of Simon in Samaria (Acts 8:10), just as the

81

first major outreach from Antioch ran foul of the false prophet Elymas in Cyprus (acts 13:6).

Of the first generation Christians it was Paul who, so far as we can tell, appears to have grasped most clearly the danger of an inspiration whose source was demonic and whose utterance could not be trusted. Wherever he is confronted with prophecy as a living force he is quick to indicate that prophetic inspiration alone is no guarantee that the inspired word is of the Spirit. So much so that *every* prophetic utterance must be subjected to careful scrutiny and evaluation. Thus in listing various charismata in 1 Cor 12:8-10 he is careful to link in close conjunction 'prophecy' and 'discernings' (*diakriseis*) of spirits'—the plural presumably indicating that each prophetic utterance should be accompanied by a process of *diakrisis*, where *diakrisis* probably has the double sense —both discerning the prophecy as to its *source* (evil spirit or Holy Spirit) *and* evaluating or interpreting the prophecy as to its *content*, what it *means* for the gathered assembly. This suggestion is confirmed by 1 Cor 14:29, where Paul's specific instruction is that if two or three prophets speak in the assembly the others should evaluate (*diakrino*) what is said —that is, again, presumably, as to its source and/or significance. So too in 1 Cor 2:13, the difficult phrase 'judging spirituals by spirituals' must include the thought that inspired speech (as well as 'the gifts bestowed on us' more generally) should always be subject to some sort of evaluation. In his earlier letter to a community which knew its full share of apocalyptic enthusiasm, he encourages them to welcome the prophetic Spirit, but at once adds, 'Test everything'—'Do not stifle inspiration, and do not despise prophetic utterances, but bring them all to the test and then keep what is good in them and avoid the bad of whatever kind' (1 Thess 5:19-22 NEB).

We should note in passing that the *Jerusalem Bible* seems to have misunderstood each of these last three passages—absolutely key passages in our present discussion. 1 Cor 2:13: 'We *teach (sunkrino)* spiritual things spiritually'—but *sunkrino* here must mean something like 'compare, or interpret', *not* 'teach'; 1 Cor 14:29: '. . . and the others *attend (diakrino)* to them'—but *diakrino* must mean something like 'judge, evaluate', *not* 'attend'; 1 Thess 5:21—'Think before you do anything'— but that is a tortuous sense for the Greek (*panta de dokimazete*)—examine everything' is much more suited to the context. Jerusalem Bible's obscuring of this function is one of its gravest weaknesses.

At the end of the first century and into the second century the emphasis and caution is the same, only much more pronounced. Prophecy is welcome and necessary, but it must be tested; it cannot claim a hearing or demand obedience without itself being submitted to some sort of evaluation. Thus 1 John 4:1–'Beleoved, do not believe every spirit, but test the spirits to see whether they are of God; for many false prophets have gone out into the world'; (Jerusalem Bible got it right here, at last–'*test* them, to see if they come from God'). Didache is even more conscious of the danger of false prophecy, and gives detailed instructions on how and when evaluation of a visiting prophet should be carried out. Not everyone who speaks 'in the spirit' is a prophet; therefore all who come 'in the name of the Lord' must be examined and tested (using the same two key verbs, *diakrino* and *dokimazo*–Did. 11:7f; 12:1). Most detailed of all is the treatment of the eleventh Mandate of Hermas, where Hermas is warned against false prophets and given careful instructions on how to test (*dokimazo*) whether a man has the divine Spirit or the spirit which is earthly, empty, powerless and foolish (Hermas, Mand. 11:7, 11, 16).

A consistent picture emerges from all this. Wherever in pre-Christian Judaism and early Christianity men have claimed that the words they spoke were inspired by God's Spirit, there has been an accompanying recognition that their claim might be false. Wherever in pre-Christian Judaism and early Christianity prophecies have been uttered 'in the name of the Lord', the need has also been stressed for some degree of discrimination and evaluation to test and discern whether they were genuine words of the Lord or not.

2. *What criteria were used in discerning, testing, evaluating prophetic utterances?*

When we look at the same range of evidence *two* criteria chiefly emerge: (a) the character of the prophet; (b) the norm of earlier revelation.

(a) *The character of the prophet.* So, for example, Isaiah and Jeremiah denounce the prophets of their own time for drunkenness, adultery, lying and encouraging immorality in others (Is 28:7; Jer 23:14). Micah denounces those who prophesy for gain or out of pique (Mc 3:5), and both Micaiah ben Imlah and Amos demonstrate how important it is for the true prophet to retain his basic independence of all but Yahweh (1 Kings 22:5ff; Amos 7:14). Likewise the criterion of Mt 7:16 focusses primarily on conduct and character–'You will know them (false prophets) by their fruits'.

Paul deals with the subject at some length in 1 Cor 12–14. Of the three criteria he employs there one of the most important is *love*: does the character of the charismatic manifest love in the exercise of his charismata?–1 Cor 13. Verses 4-7 are clearly polemical in intent. The Corinthian charismatics, exulting in their experiences of angelic speech (glossolalia) and the extent of their prophetic powers, had evidently become all that love is not—impatient, unkind, jealous, boastful, arrogant, rude, etc. Such a loveless character was sufficient indication that the *charis* (grace) behind their *charisma* was not 'the grace of the Lord Jesus Christ' (cf. Gal 5:16-24). Similarly 1 John offers various 'tests of life' which will demonstrate the reality of the community's fellowship and their common participation in the Spirit. The one which John seems to emphasise most strongly is love of the brethren—2:7-11; 3:11-18; 4:7-12, 20f; 5:2; 2 John 5f.

Didache urges that all wandering charismatics or visiting missionaries should be tested (12:1)—prophets are particularly mentioned, but teachers and apostles have to be tested too. The principal criterion is again the test of conduct—'It is by their conduct that the false prophet and the (true) prophet can be distinguished' (11:8). Examples of conduct which fails the test include, asking for money, even when the request or command is made 'in the spirit' (11:6, 12), and living off the community for more than two or three days (11:5; 12:2ff). Here conduct is seen as evidence of motivation: the true apostle, prophet, teacher will be untrammeled with possessions and constantly driven to move on by his missionary compulsion.

Similarly in Hermas the chief criterion is the character of the prophet's conduct and life—'Therefore test by his life and his works the man who says that he is moved by the Spirit' (11:16). The false prophet is ambitious and greedy for honour; he is bold, shameless and talks too much; he lives in luxury and accepts money for his prophecies; he avoids meeting with the congregation as a whole where he would be unmasked by the righteous, and associates instead with the 'double-minded' and the 'empty', meeting with them privately to minister to them (11:12-13).

(b) *The norm of earlier revelation.* The Old Testament writers found it difficult to formulate an adequate test of false prophecy. Several settled on one form or another of the test of fulfilment and non-fulfilment. Second Isaiah uses this criterion repeatedly (eg. 44:7f). And Jeremiah offers a rather more refined version—'If a prophet foretells prosperity, when his words come true it will be known that the Lord has sent him' (Jer 28:9). The most famous expression of this test is the classic statement of Dt 18:22—'When the word spoken by the prophet in the name of the Lord is not fulfilled and does not come true, it is not a word spoken by the Lord. The prophet has spoken presumptuously; do not hold him in awe'. But Deuteronomy also recognised that *fulfilment* of a prophet's prediction is *not* an adequate test— *false* prophecies may be fulfilled as well. The more basic criterion is *loyalty to Yahweh*—'If he (the prophet says, "Let us go after other gods" which you have not known, "and let us serve them", you shall not listen to that prophet. . .' (Dt 13:1ff). This is the first attempt to formulate the criterion of past revelation—loyalty to Yahweh as he has revealed himself in the past serves as a criterion to test claims of revelation in the present. In fact however the Old Testament never really solved the problem of false prophecy satisfactorily or finally.

The criterion of past revelation is first formally enunciated by Paul. In 1 Cor 12—14 the first criterion he offers for testing inspired utterance is that of the kerygmatic tradition: 1 Cor 12:3—'No one speaking by the Spirit of God says, "Jesus is cursed"; and no one can say "Jesus is Lord" except by the Holy Spirit'. Here the test is a basic statement of the gospel—'Jesus is Lord'—probably the basic confession of hellenistic Christianity (cf. Rom 10:9; 1 Cor 8:6; 2 Cor 4:5. etc). This gives the test of 1 Cor 12:3 a particular importance. But probably in Paul's mind it is only one example of the larger criterion of past revelation/kerygmatic tradition; as he makes it clear elsewhere, if *any* inspired utterance runs counter to the gospel by which they were converted it is to be rejected (Gal 1:8; 2 Cor 11:4; cf. 2 Thess 2:15; Col 2:6).

In 1 John the test by which the Spirit of God may be recognised is the confession that Jesus Christ has come in the flesh; whereas the spirit of antichrist refuses to make this confession (1 John 4:1ff; cf. 2:22f; 4:15; 5:1). Here again we have the criterion of kerygmatic tradition, of past revelation. Similarly in Didache, that which is already accepted as 'the truth' serves as a criterion by which charismatic utterances can be tested—the teaching which has already been received previously. If the prophet, apostle or teacher does not teach 'the truth' he is to be ignored (11:1f).

In Hermas the criterion of past revelation is not so clearly presented, but is there implicitly. The false prophet is an empty man who responds with empty words to empty questioners (11:2f). 'Empty' (*kenos*) is obviously a key word in Hermas's understanding of false prophecy (11: 3, 11, 13, 15, 17). What he means by it is not altogther clear. But he also describes the false prophet's clientele as 'double-minded, empty of the truth and ignorant' (11:1f, 4), in contrast to those who are 'strong in the faith of the Lord, clothed with the truth'. Consequently we may infer that the *kenos* was one who was not well-versed in the faith, the kergymatic and confessional truth about Christianity; and further, that false prophecy was revealed as empty precisely by its failure to express or accord with the basic message of Christian faith. That is to say, once again we have in fact the criterion of past revelation.

(c) *Community benefit.* For the sake of completeness we should simply mention the other main criterion which is used by Paul—*oiko-dome* (edification)—a test applied regularly throughout 1 Cor 14. In particular it is this test which demonstrates with finality for Paul that of the two most prominent types of inspired utterance in the Corinthian assembly, prophecy is superior to glossolalia; for glossolalia is a purely private personal affair between the individual and God, whereas through prophecy God speaks to the whole congregation and builds it up by opening it more and more to God (14:1-5, 12, 17, 24f). So too it is the overruling need that all things are to be done in the assembly 'for edification' which makes evaluation of prophetic utterance indispensable (14:29) and which presumably provides the means of evaluation (cf. 8:1; 10:23)—since for Paul prophecy is only a charisma insofar as it is also a means of serving (*diakonia*) the community (12:4f). This criterion is probably also implicit in 1 John, Didache and Hermas, but nowhere else is it so clearly formulated as in Paul.

To sum up then, not only was the danger of false prophecy regularly recognised within the religion of Israel and early Christianity; but, in addition, wherever this danger was recognised, the need to test *all* prophecy was also recognised and appropriate criteria were sought. Indeed, the energy with which the problem of false prophecy was tackled and the variety of tests applied show just how serious was the threat that false prophecy posed to the prophetic vitality of Israelite and early Christian religion. The two chief criteria which have emerged regularly are (a) the criterion of present character and conduct—for example, immoral conduct, loveless action, abuse of hospitality and selling prophetic oracles as a commodity—these all fail the test—the life of the prophet must be in accord with the message he brings; and (b) the criterion of past revelation—expressed variously in terms of loyalty to Yahweh, kerygmatic tradition, the teaching given from the beginning, the faith, the truth—the inspired utterance must not gainsay that which has already demonstrated its authenticity as divine revelation. These two criteria are hardly surprising; they are the most obviously tests to be used in a religion which is of a high moral character and which stems from key revelatory events in history.

One other point should be noted here—viz. the frequency with which prophets and prophetic utterances were tested only to be *rejected* within early Christianity. For example, Paul admonishes the Thessalonians in effect to reject the prophecy that the day of the Lord has already come (2 Thess 2:2)—just as in the Little Apocalypse disciples are warned to reject those who say, 'I am he', 'Look, here is the Christ', and so on (Mk 13:6, 21). In 1 Cor 12:3 and 1 John 2:22 the test of past revelation determines that the inspired utterances 'Jesus be cursed',

'Jesus is not the Christ' must be emphatically rejected. The test of character disqualifies the charismatics in Mt 7:21ff even though they prophesy in Jesus' name. For similar reasons the prophet who says 'Give me money' or some such thing must be rejected, even though he speaks 'in the spirit' (Did. 11:12). And in Acts 21:4ff Paul apparently rejected the prophetic instruction *not* to go to Jerusalem—even though given 'through the Spirit'. In short, the testing of prophetic utterances was by no means a mere formality in early Christianity. When someone spoke under inspiration the community did not simply listen gape-mouthed and accept it without question as a word of the exalted Christ. On the contrary churches seem to have been very conscious of the very real danger of false inspiration, of false prophecy. And a great many prophetic oracles were tested and *found wanting*—to be rejected either as to source or as to content.

I began by drawing attention to the importance of this area of study both for research into the New Testament Gospel traditions and for the Pentecostal movement. The relevance of our findings thus far to the form critical method I have dealt with elsewhere.[4] In what follows I direct my remarks more to the Pentecostal movement and charismatic renewal.

3. *Who was responsible for exercising the gift of discernment?*

As we noted at the beginning, the importance of this gift has not been fully recognised by either radical New Testament scholarship or by Pentecostalism. I have to add however that this is much less true of Catholicism and of Catholic Pentecostals. In the 1960s the charismatic movement was influenced directly by classic Pentecostalism and so took over Pentecostal theology without much significant variation But some Catholic Pentecostals, much less dependent on classic Pentecostalism and drawing on their own tradition much more extensively, have been quicker to recognise the importance of discernment. Here, of course, they have had the valuable statement of Vatican II on the Church (*Lumen Gentium*), particularly the second half of paragraph 12 which draws attention to the charismata apportioned to each member of the body of Christ, and which ends by stressing the importance of exercising discrimination in relation to these gifts:

> The decision on their genuineness (the spiritual gifts) and on the organisation of their exercise rests with the men who are over the Church, and whose specific competence lies, not in quenching the Spirit, but in testing everything and in holding fast what is good (cf. 1 Thess 5:12, 19-21).

It is worth noting in this context that the recent book by Thomas Flynn, *The Charismatic Renewal and the Irish Experience* (Hodder 1974) quotes or refers to this passage no less than three times (pp. 128, 139, 154)—first in the Statement of Pope Paul VI, then in the interview with Archbishop Hayes of Halifax, Nova Scotia, and again in the Statement of the Theological Basis of the Catholic Charismatic Movement, by Kilian McDonnell. McDonnell indeed recognises that, 'Discernment of spirits is one of the major ongoing problems of the renewal' (p. 153). So to that extent I must clearly qualify my statement about the failure to recognise the importance of testing inspired utterances—at least some in the Catholic Charismatic Renewal recognise its importance well enough.

However, I should not qualify my opening statement too far. For I find myself asking whether the statement in *Lumen Gentium* is adequate—particularly whether it is adequate in its exegesis. I am thinking here mainly with reference to our present question—*Who* is responsible for the exercise of this gift? It is quite clear that for *Lumen Gentium* the exercise of the gift of discernment belongs to the specific competence of 'the men who are over the Church'. Archbishop Hayes indeed recalls Pope Paul VI's statement in these terms:

> (He said) that it is up to the Bishop to be the discerner of the Spirits. In fact he called the discernment by the Bishop 'The charism of charisms', and he said that it is the Bishop who has to test all things and hold fast to that which is good. . . (to) encourage the movements that the Bishop perceives or discerns to be of the Holy Spirit' (p. 139).

My point is, that insofar as this explanation of the gift of discernment claims to be rooted in the New Testament it is based on a *wrong* exegesis, or at least on a very inadequate and forced exegesis. The one passage that *Lumen Gentium* cites is 1 Thess 5:12, 19-21. Now, certainly 1 Thess 5:12 could be taken as a reference to an embryonic hierarchical set-up—'those who labour among you and care for you in the Lord and admonish you' though for myself I can see neither hierarchy nor formal authority here (see below). But even if 1 Thess 5:12 could be taken as a reference to such leadership, it is almost impossible to understand 5:19-21 as addressed to that leadership. It is quite clear that those who are addressed in 5:12 and again 14ff are the 'brethren'—that is, the community at large, as a whole. It is the community as a whole that Paul calls on not to quench the Spirit, not to despise prophecy, but to test everything. . . (5:19-21). That is to say, it is almost impossible to avoid the exegetical conclusion that the gift of discernment is the prerogative of *all*—not to be exercised by just a few, but to be exercised by the whole community.[5]

This conclusion is borne out by the other passages which deal with the gift of discernment. 1 Cor 2:12-16—the 'we' of whom Paul speaks here must refer to every believer, since (all) believers are by definition those who 'have received the Spirit which is from God'—the Spirit being given in order 'that we might know/understand the gifts bestowed on us by God'. It is the same group who exercise the gift of discernment in v. 13—'comparing the spiritual gifts (which we already possess) with the spiritual gifts (as we receive them) and judging them thereby; or 'interpreting spiritual truths by means of spiritual words'; or 'interpreting spiritual truths to those who have the Spirit' (NEB). Again in vv. 14-15, who is it who 'judges or discerns' the things of the Spirit, who 'judges or discerns' (*anakrino*) all things?—the spiritual man (*ho pneumatikos*) —that is, the Christian, the one who has received the Spirit. It is abundantly clear from the context that Paul has no thought here of 'the spiritual man' as an inner circle, or ruling group, formal or otherwise. On the contrary, it is precisely that kind of elitism (here charismatic elitism) which he is arguing against. Since all believers, or at least all believers who walk by the Spirit and live according to love, are *pneumatikoi*, men of the Spirit, so it follows, inevitably in Paul's mind, that all have the responsiblity of exercising discernment in matters pretaining to the Spirit—not least inspired utterance.

In 1 Cor 14:29 his recommendation may be slightly different—'Let two or three prophets speak, and let the others weigh what is said'. Who are 'the others' who are to weigh (*diakrino*) what is said under inspiration? The most obvious answer is 'the other prophets'. In other words here at least Paul envisages the prime responsiblity for evaluating prophecy as falling on the prophets—those who prophesy regularly. I suspect that the following direction with regard to women relates to the same subject (bearing in mind that women also prophesied in the Pauline assembly—1 Cor 11:5). That is to say, the reason why Paul urged silence upon them was probably because they were taking part in the process of discernment and evaluation—making irrelevent or not very helpful comments, sidetracking the discussion with questions which missed the point, etc. It this is so, then the implication is that the process of evaluation and judgment was not in fact confined to the prophets, but that the prophets were at the centre of a discussion in which all members could take part with only the women told to restrain themselves.

The only other New Testament passage of immediate relevance is 1 John 4:1ff. Who is responsible for testing the spirits here? The answer

89

does not become immediately apparent from the passage itself, and we have to depend on our wider understanding of church and ministry in the Gospel and First Epistle of John. And here we must simply observe that John seems to have *no* concept of special ministry let alone of office reserved for a few—even the group round Jesus in the Gospel are never 'the twelve' or 'apostles', but simple 'the disciples', representative of the disciples of all succeeding generations. And in 1 John the same is true. Rather each *individual* is united directly with Christ, feeds directly on Christ, is taught directly by the Spirit—everything is seen in terms of the individual's immediate relationship to God through the Spirit and the word.[6] Consequently the responsiblity of 1 John 4:1ff is laid not on any specific ministry, or hiearchy, or even on the whole church as such, but on each individual member; as each member rejoices so fully in the immediacy of his relationship with God, so each must know how to guard against spiritual deception both in his own case and when he encounters a brother.

To sum up then, while Catholicism and Catholic Pentecostals do recognise the importance of the gift of discernment, unlike radical form criticism or classic Pentecostalism, they nevertheless have neglected it insofar as they have failed fully to understand Paul's teaching on it. In particular they have failed to appreciate where in Paul's and John's scheme of things the responsibility for exercising this gift lies— not solely with a limited group, though in particular instances probably initially with those who are most experienced in charisma being evaluated; but otherwise the responsibility lies with the whole community, and with each individual believer.

4. *How was the gift of discernment to be exercised?*

Here we come to the heart of the matter—how?—the point being that it was not a simple matter of pronouncing Yes or No, Right or Wrong! It was inevitably a much more delicate process altogether. This is no doubt one of the main reasons why the gift has been neglected today: it is so difficult and time-consuming to exercise. The fact is, of course, that whether consciously or not in every case some process of discernment or evaluation is being followed. It may be wholly naive and credulous, or it may be stiflingly pedantic; but each time a claim to inspiration is made, the community and/or the individuals who hear it do make up their minds one way or other about it. If then evaluation is inevitable, it is all the more necessary that the gift of discernment be taken seriously, and what the New Testament writers say about it, particularly Paul's understanding of it as a *gift*—that is to say, properly understood, discernment as to source and significance of an inspired utterance was something given by God and neither contrived nor manipulated by man. But what did this mean in practice? How did Paul envisage the gift being received and exercised? Here I can only sketch briefly the outlines of the answer which seems to emerge from Paul. Above all, when we hear in mind the nature of the chief criteria of evaluation and the *community's* responsibility to exercise the gift, what becomes evident is that discernment involves a *dialectical process*, that the gift is not independent of the community's careful and sensitive use of the criteria.

(a) *The dialectic of liberty.* The first criterion was character and conduct: the inspired utterance must accord with and promote a loving character and loving conduct. But what is loving conduct? It was certainly not to be determined by the straightforward application of a ready-made yardstick or by reference to a rule book. That might serve in some extreme cases, as in the case of incest in 1 Cor 5. But what about the very large grey area in between? What we have to remember here is that for Paul a believer's conduct is now determined not primarily by a written code, but by the immediate direction of the Spirit: '... we no longer serve under the old written code but in the new life of the Spirit' (Rom 7:6; 2 Cor 3:6). This of course is why he was able to urge his converts to walk by the Spirit, be led by the Spirit, etc. (as in Rom 8:4, 14; Gal 5:16, 18, 25). In other words, so far as Paul was concerned, loving conduct was something much more spontaneous than can be tested by simple reference to the rule book and precedent—it was much more in the nature of *obedience to an inward compulsion.* In particular we may note that discernment also played a role here—in the individual's own assessment of what the Spirit required of him in a particular instance—discernment here being understood as a divine enabling to know what God's will was in a particular instance without reference to the written code. I often quote the words of Cullmann at this point:

> The working of the Holy Spirit shows itself chiefly in the 'testing' (*dokimazein*), that is *the capacity of forming the correct Christian ethical judgment at each given moment...* This 'testing' is the key to all Christian ethics... Certainty of moral judgment in the concrete sense is in the last analysis the one great fault that the Holy Spirit ... produces in the individual man.[7]

Now, the question is, what happened when a course of action decided thus by one believer *clashed* with the actions of others? — when the 'strong' clashed with the 'weak' on the question of whether it is right to eat meat or to refrain, to observe certain days as special or treat all days as the same (Rom 14)? What happened when Peter and Paul disagreed over the right course of action at Antioch (Gal 2:11ff)? What happened when those of the Gentile mission clashed with the Christians from Jerusalem over circumcision (Acts 15; Gal 2:1-10)? No single answer to all these emerges from the Pauline literature. In some cases the 'strong' should restrict their liberty for the sake of the 'weak' (1 Cor 8; 10: 23ff)—so Paul apparently circumcised Timothy because he had one Jewish parent, and for the sake of the Jewish Christians (Acts 16:3). In other cases the 'strong' should insist on their liberty since it is the liberty of the gospel itself—so Paul refused to circumcise Titus despite the Jewish Christians (Gal 2:3-5). But who should have given way in the dispute at Antioch and why? Who did give way? How was the issue resolved? We do not know. The point is that the use of the first criterion necessarily involves the *dialectic of liberty*—where there has to be a most careful weighing up of the different factors, a dialectic between the liberty of community to call for conformity and the liberty of individual not to conform, and in it all a prayerful waiting before God, open to the *gift* of discrnment, open, that is, to a judgment which may be unexpected and even unlooked for.

(b) *The dialectic of revelation.* The second criterion was the norm of past revelation. But again the use of this criterion and the process of evaluation is necessarily dialectical. It cannot simply be a matter of referring back to the already accepted tradition, to past revelation. For what precisely is at stake here is what is the *normative* revelation for *here and now.* What has to be assessed is precisely the claims of old revelation over against those of new. It is not simply a matter of referring back to tradition with the recognition that the tradition has to be *interpreted.* It may be that the process of evaluation has to reach the conclusion that the old tradition, the old revelation is no longer relevant and has been superseded.

Let me give some examples from the New Testament. (1) Initially the first believers in Jerusalem seem to have stuck firmly to the temple and to Jerusalem. Only with the Hellenists and Stephen in particular was that continuing loyalty, the loyalty of tradition and to tradition, called in question. But then it was called in question very sharply—the temple being attacked as idolatrous (Acts 7:48-50).[8] Who was right in this case? The local Jewish Christians were holding fast to the temple in accordance with the criterion of past revelation. Stephen and company, apparently following up the logic of some words of Jesus about the temple (Mk 14:58; Jn 2:19; Acts 6:14), believed that new revelation had superseded the old. How should the criterion of past revelation have been applied there? (2) Paul stresses that his gospel came direct from God—from the 'revelation of Jesus Christ' (Gal 1:12). But he also maintains that it was consistent with the earlier formulations of the gospel, and that it was accepted by the pillar apostles—though evidently not by all of the Jerusalem Christians (Gal 2:1-10). What was at stake here was clearly Paul's interpretation of the 'revelation of Jesus Christ' as implying, necessitating a *law-free* mission to the Gentiles. In other words, Paul's was an understanding of tradition as always open to a new revelation from God, a revelation which might reshape the whole of earlier revelation and point in a radically new direction.[9] (3) In 1 John 4:1ff the test of kerygmatic tradition is not an original form of the gospel. The affirmation 'Jesus Christ came in the flesh' is clearly a late first century confessional response to the threat of docetism (cf. 1 John 5:6ff). No doubt in John's mind that confession was wholly consistent with 'that which you have heard from the beginning' (2:24; 3:11). The point is, that the test used is not itself the past revelation—it is the earlier revelation already interpreted and reformulated in relation to new situations emerging and in relation to claims of further revelation. The test used is itself the product of the dialectical process of weighing new revelation against old.

In all these cases we see the dialectic of revelation—the recognition that in some instances past revelation will be normative, in others that past revelation will have to be regarded as superseded, no longer relevant to the present. Once again, if the gift of discernment is to be experienced as a gift and exercised as a gift these questions must remain open and the possibility accepted of either judgment being reached.

(c) *The dialectic of authority.* If we look now at the process of assessment from the angle of those responsible to exercise the gift of discernment we see again the dialectical nature of the whole process. For as the criteria do not provide us with a simple yardstick of judgment, so the achievement of an authoritative assessment is not left to a few members of the community, far less vested in a recognisable office. As E. Kasemann has rightly insisted, so far as the Pauline community is concerned, authority resides in or belongs to the *act* of ministry itself—it resides neither in the person nor in an office, but in the particular charisma itself.[10] Moreoever, the concomitant responsibility to evaluate that charisma is laid upon all.

Now this fact is true of all ministry, of all charismata in the Pauline vision of community. It is true even of the *apostle*. In the Pauline church the apostle has authority, in part at least, because the community had already evaluated and approved that authority—their conversion under his preaching was in effect their acceptance of his authority, their very existence as the body of Christ was itself an expression of his

93

authority. That is why Paul could adopt an authoritative stance towards one of his churches: they could not gainsay his commission, for they themselves were proof of it—1 Cor 9:2: 'If to others I am not an apostle, at least I am to you; for you are the seal of my apostleship in the Lord'. Paul could also lay down the law about the gospel or the tradition—but we have already noted the dialectic involved in his authority at that point. Elsewhere in his letters, most significantly, Paul does not lay down the law or demand compliance, but only offers his opinion (1 Cor 7:25, 40). To be sure, he is confident of his own inspiration, but that does not exempt him from submitting that opinion to the assessment of the rest. On the contrary, it makes it all the more necessary that they should evaluate it—even an apostle may experience false prophecy. So too, even where he is certain that his instructions are a 'command of the Lord', he still does not expect them to be obeyed merely on his word; first they must be *recognised* as the Lord's command and then obeyed on that basis.[11]

And if an apostle's authority was not something which stood independently of all evaluation, how much more with the other ministries. Prophecy, as we have seen, always had to be evaluated, not least by the community. The authority of the teacher was the authority of his tradition, and that needed to be interpreted, and so the interpretation to be evaluated. Other regular ministries like those of Stephanas at Corinth likewise depended to some extent at least on the evaluation of the community—the community had the responsibility to recognise the authority which already belonged to their ministry, and only when they did so could that ministry have its full effectiveness (1 Cor 16:15-18; 1 Thess 5:12f). This responsibility of the whole community in exercising discernment is most clearly seen in 1 Corinthians—where it was manifestly the church as a whole, and not just some leadership group within it, whose responsibility it was to exercise proper restraint and authority in such matters as resolving differences between brothers such as might end in court, ordering the common meal and Lord's Supper so that none might be neglected, and organising the collection for the poor at Jerusalem.[12] This responsiblity is perhaps most typified by the congregation's 'Amen' in 1 Cor 14:16. From what Paul says, it was clearly not merely a formal liturgical assent, for it could not be given unless the church understood what was said, that is, it could not be given unless it expressed the church's understanding and response. In other words, the 'Amen' expressed the community's assessment of the inspired utterance.

In short, the exercise of *authority* in assessing any claim to inspiration is dialectic in nature—a dialectic between the founding apostle, the particular act of ministry in word and deed, those who manifest

94

that particular gift regularly, and the community as a whole. If then we are to follow the guidelines which emerge from Paul's letters, it is in and through this process that the community as a whole must seek the best evaluation. That is, since again I say discernment is itself a gift, those responsible for evaluating a charisma must seek in and through this process to be open to the emergence of some pointer or other towards the right assessment of the charisma, perhaps some unexpected pointer, and must be ready to evaluate the different and competing claims to authority in relation to each case and its particular situation.

Conclusion

It seems to me that the Charismatic Movement *and* the Church which still embraces it stand at a crossroads. The question which confronts both is: Can the Church adapt sufficiently to *continue* to hold the Charismatic Movement within it? The dangers are obvious: on the one hand that the Charismatic Movement will sooner or later cut loose and drift away from the older churches, or perhaps will be repressed to some degree within the older churches and explode into a new life and forms much more independent of the older denominations—as in the case of early Methodism; on the other hand, the danger that the Church will sooner or later, quickly or slowly, stifle the vitality and enthusiasm of the Charismatic Movement and all that will be left in another twenty years will be a wide scatter of middle-aged Christians sighing sadly over the exciting days long gone.

It seems to me that both the Charismatic Movement and the greater Church will only be able to steer their joint course between that particular Scylla and Charybdis if they recognise the crucial importance of discernment of spirits and take with sufficient seriousness the ongoing problem which it poses. In particular it seems to me that those dangers will be escaped only if all involved recognise the *dialectic* of discernment—the dialectic of liberty, the dialectic of revelation, the dialectic of authority. Only if the Church is really willing to listen to the Charismatic Movement's claims of a new revelation, of a liberty more fully perceived, of an authority more widely exercised, and only where it is *possible* for such claims to be fully *accepted* by the Church, only then can the Church hope to retain the Charismatic Movement. But likewise, only where the Charismatic Movement is willing to submit such claims to the wider community of the Church, only where it is prepared for some of them to be evaluated and found wanting, only then can the Charismatic Movement hope to remain within the wider Church and influence its future course. This is the dialectic of discernment. This is what is involved in the gift of discernment, so badly neglected in the

95

past for the sake of Christianity as a whole and its future over the next generation.

NOTES

1. R. Bultmann, *The History of the Synoptic Tradition*, ET Blackwell, 1963, pp. 127f.
2. E. Kasemann, *Essays on New Testament Themes*, ET SCM Press, 1964, p. 60.
3. I have attempted to demonstrate this in detail in *Baptism in the Holy Spirit*, SCM Press 1970, and *Jesus and the Spirit*, SCM Press 1975.
4. J. D. G. Dunn, 'Prophetic "I"—Sayings and the Jesus Tradition: the Importance of Testing Prophetic Utterances within Early Christianity, in *NTS* 24 (1977-78) 175-198.
5. Dr Robert Murray, S.J., has kindly drawn my attention to the fact that since Vatican II the text referred to here is being interpreted within Roman Catholicism not only in terms of episcopal authority, and that a new style of decision-taking through communal discernment has developed in many circles, both clerical, lay and mixed, whereby the leader (even bishops in many cases) takes part within the group and does not take the decision alone. Many of my Roman Catholic readers will know of examples involving diocesan pastoral councils, chapters of religious orders and charismatic communities.
6. See Dunn, *Jesus and the Spirit*, pp. 354f.
7. O. Cullmann, *Christ and Time*, ET SCM Press 1962[3], p. 228.
8. See Dunn, *Unity and Diversity in the New Testament*, SCM Press 1977, pp. 271f.
9. Ibid, pp. 66f., 77f.
10. E. Kasemann, 'Ministry and Community in the New Testament,' in *Essays*, pp. 78, 83; see also Dunn, *Jesus and the Spirit*, p. 291.
11. See more fully Dunn, *Jesus and the Spirit*, pp. 275-280.
12. Ibid., pp. 291-93.

THE HOLY SPIRIT AND THE LIFE
OF THE SPIRIT TODAY

Patrick Corcoran, C.M.

'The Holy Spirit', the 'Life of the Spirit', and 'Today' have each provided material for many books. It is perhaps, foolhardy to speak of them all in a single essay. I am aware that I am offering points for discussion rather than solving problems. I hope to reflect on some aspects of the relation between doctrine and devotion: I hope to illustrate where theology can help and sometimes theologians can hinder devotion to the Holy Spirit. I am not discussing, except very incidentally, different emphases of the Churches of the East or the Churches of the Reformation. I am speaking I hope, out of my own tradition.

An idea whose time has come.

According to Victor Hugo 'Nothing is so powerful as an idea whose time has come'. Today this would seem to be true of the Holy Spirit. Within living memory there has been no period like the last ten years when the Holy Spirit has been so much in the public eye. He has become a superstar—one whose musical has not yet been written—but nonetheless a superstar. People talk and write freely of a New Pentecost, a new Age of the Spirit, the evident signs of the Spirit. His day is considered to have come because in some way he is the precise remedy for the specific ills of our age. He is considered particularly apt to re-vitalise a Church which has lost its snap, pop, and crackle—so the argument runs. It is urged that he, in particular, will ensure that renewal we have all been talking about for so long.

Pentecostalism

Pentecostalism has contributed to the public image of the Holy Spirit. Movements claiming special access to the Holy Spirit are not new. One may recall the Montanists in the early centuries, various exponents in the Middle Ages, groups at the Reformation, Quakers, American Protestants in the early nineteenth century, Buchmanites in the thirties and forties. What is new is the emergence of groups in the

Catholic Church in the past decade. These originated from contact with Protestant Pentecostals. In the interim these groups have had a quiet change of name. More frequently nowadays one hears 'charismatic', 'renewal', 'prayer' used to identify these groups. This change of name is an effort to disavow the excesses of the Pentecostals and avoid the criticisms that may be directed at them. However some of the family features persist, and so do the criticisms. The Canadian Bishops, for example, have issued a document which falls into two parts. The first part outlines goals that these Catholic groups might achieve. The second underlines certain pitfalls that have not been avoided sufficiently. Such pitfalls are the seeking of marvels, overemphasis on 'belonging', emotionalism, fundamentalism, self-centredness of groups, false ecumenism. Harsher criticisms have been voiced both inside and outside the Church. My concern here is not primarily with these groups, though one can hardly avoid mentioning them when talking about the Holy Spirit today. It is not my concern to follow in detail the pluses or minuses of these groups though certain reservations will appear en route. My concern is principally with the Holy Spirit and devotion to him.

A Vacuum

The 'charismatic' movement could be seen, and is seen by some as filling a vacuum that has occured in our time. Part of this vacuum is an insufficient devotion to the Holy Spirit. Leo XIII in his encyclical *Divinum Illud Munus* lamented the fact that the Holy Spirit was not better appreciated. Like many a papal encyclical before and since its message went largely unheeded. This was due to a breakdown in the chain of command. Unless doctrine and devotion are preached in due measure they tend to disappear, or by a kind of Gresham's law, they yield to couterfeit. Preaching, of course, is dependent on theology and theology (or the teaching of theology) has much to answer for. Many priests of yesteryear experienced difficulty in preaching about the Holy Spirit. The would recall the 'theology' of the Holy Spirit as a series of footnotes here and there in different areas of theology. My own conviction is that the classical theology of the Holy Spirit was more versatile than we realised or than we made it appear. I am not saying that priests now or in the foreseeable future will find it easy to do justice to the Holy Spirit. Theologically, the Holy Spirit like the mystery of the Trinity is a difficult subject. There are difficulties not only in expressing the doctrine, but also in expressing our devotion appropriately.

A Theological Minimum

Of course it is not necessary to have mastered all the intricacies of trinitarian theology to speak of the Holy Spirit and to practise devotion to him. On the other hand there is a bare theological minimum that one cannot neglect. I may express this theological minimum in this way: the Holy Spirit is a Person of the Holy Trinity, he is not the only Person of the Trinity, and he is given to us in an incarnational way. One might leave matters here were it not that these points are not simple and obvious to all.

The Person of the Spirit

I would hardly need to stress the first point that the Holy Spirit is a Person of the Trinity were it not that some influential writers question the use of the term 'person' in the Trinity. Karl Barth, in particular, and Karl Rahner in a degree, emphasise the dangers of the term 'person' and prefer the expression 'modes of existence', or 'modes of subsistence' to indicate the Father, the Son, and the Holy Spirit. I do not question the excellent credentials of this expression: it has a thoroughly good patristic origin, and at a certain level of rarefaction the qualifications it offers are important. In some popular writing there has been a minor epidemic of rejection of the term 'person'—no doubt due to the influence of Barth. H. Berkhof[1] cautions us against 'this confused and confusing term', and quotes M. Kahler 'To conceive of the Spirit as a Person in relation to God would contradict the classical doctrine of the Trinity.'

If the Holy Spirit is not a Person it is an easy step to regarding him as something less, as something impersonal, no longer even as a *modus existendi*, but a *modus loquendi*. Pannenberg, revamping some ideas of Teilhard speaks of the Spirit as a field of force.[2] Many centuries earlier Gregory of Nazianzen was confronted with the error of those who thought the Holy Spirit was simply an energy (*Oratio Theologica* V). Troeltsch in the nineteenth century (to name but one) saw the Holy Trinity as a working formula to designate God's activity in the world.[3] Anyone familiar with trinitarian theology will know the genuine hesitations that great minds have had about the term 'person'. Augustine said he used it because otherwise he would have to remain silent. Anselm later expresses his bafflement when he exclaimed, *Tres nescio quid*. We know that the term must be kept on a tight leash: otherwise we end up with triplets, and not a Trinity—with three manikins as Calvin said.

If we are to reject terms simply because they are open to misunderstanding then we must cease to speak about the Trinity, or for that matter about anything else. The most dangerous terms in the whole trinitarian vocabulary are 'Father' and 'Son'. They have been the cause of endless trouble. So will any other terms which are used of God without being sufficiently refined and qualified. 'Modus existendi' and 'modus subsistendi' underline some of the qualifications we must keep in mind. However I think that terms, or the persons who use them, come of age, and the term 'person' is indispensable in the Trinity. As Lonergan has rightly noted regarding Barth it is difficult to have a dialogue with a 'modus subsistendi'. 'Person' may not be a biblical term, but the reality that it expresses is biblical. What the term 'person' conveys about the Holy Spirit has been expressed long ago by Gregory of Nyssa: 'A Being after the likeness of God's Word existing as a Person, able to will, self-moved, efficient, ever choosing the good, and for its every purpose having power concurrent with its will.'[4] Person, more than any of these other terms that have been suggested comes closest to doing justice to St John's final wod about God: God is Love.

Not alone the Spirit

The second point I can make in the words of John Bunyan:

> Some think the love of the Father and the blood of the Son will do without the holiness of the Spirit of God; but they are deceived... There is a sort that thinks the holiness of the Spirit is sufficient of itself; but they (if they had it) are deceived also; for it must be the grace of the Father, the grace of the Son, and the grace of the Spirit that must save them.[5]

I shall have to return to the point Bunyan makes—the tendency to a monism of the Holy Spirit, the tendency to see the Spirit alone.

In an Incarnational Way

The third point I should like to make is that the Holy Spirit is given to us in an incarnational way. This means first of all that the revelation of the Holy Spirit—as the mystery of the Trinity—is given in its fullness in and through the Incarnation. 'No one has ever seen God; the only Son who is the bosom of the Father, He has made Him known' (Jn 1: 18). The mission of the Spirit is bound up with the Incarnation—in bringing about the Incarnation, and in assuring the follow-through of the Incarnation, in bringing to fruition the work of our Saviour to the end of time. This may seem obvious enough though I shall have to recall some aspects of it later. What needs more explanation, perhaps, is the incarnational character of our relationship with the Holy Spirit in our spiritual life.

The Life of the Spirit

I am aware of the risk of endeavouring to encapsulate in a few words a theology of the spiritual life which has developed over many centuries, through a subtle and chequered history. Basically, the spiritual life is about grasp—God's grasp of us, and our grasp of God. I am trying, here, to paraphrase St Paul: *si quomodo comprehendam in quo et comprehensus sum* (Phil 3:12). It is important to remember that God's grasp is prior: as St John writes, he loved us first. It is important too that our grasp close on the extended hand of God. It is said that the grip of a drowning man is very strong but however strong it is, it is useless if it simply closes on itself.

Put in another way the life of the Spirit is not an indian rope trick in which we improve on the original by climbing up the rope. Rather it is a Jacob's ladder let down to us from Heaven. It is the whole mystery of God, the Incarnation, the whole Gospel, the Church and the sacraments. Indeed it reaches down to our efforts for as St Augustine says: *sua dona coronabit, non merita nostra (Enarr. in Ps 70)*.

The spiritual life or the life of the Spirit is about our relationship with God. This relationship is not exclusive but comprehensive—one in which we relate to all else in, and with, and through God. Augustine expresses this well. 'One should relate all one's life to the recall, the vision and the love of the sovereign Trinity, to recall it, to contemplate it and rejoice in it.'[6] He gives another piece of advice which is directly about the Son, but is applicable to the Holy Spirit as well. 'The Son is sent to each one when He is known and perceived by anyone as far as He can be known and perceived by the capacity of the soul.'[7] The question, then, is: what is the capacity of the soul to know and perceive the Holy Spirit and to relate directly to him? It seems to me that efforts to answer this question over the centuries are studded with great expectations and great reservations.

The Face of the Spirit?

The great expectations arise from people who try to get on terms with the Holy Spirit in a way that is not possible. Some look for a polaroid camera picture of the Holy Spirit which can be developed in ten seconds flat. In some degree this itch is in us all. Philip spoke for us all when he said 'Show us the Father and it is enough'. And Jesus spoke to us all when he said 'Who sees me sees the Father', and this is true for the Holy Spirit no less than for the Father.

Many writers have great reservations about seeing the face of the Spirit but some seem to urge the 'faceless' element too far. They stress the 'anonymity', the 'incognito' of the Spirit, and even speak of the 'kenosis' of the Spirit.[8] The Holy Spirit is like a character in a play who has an important part to play, perhaps even a determining part, but never appears on-stage, and never should. The Spirit is a *quo* but not a *quod*. He is the agent of our progress but never the *terminus ad quem.*

> The indwelling of the Spirit involves the indwelling of Christ; consequently the indwelling of Christ is inseparable from the quickening. But the Spirit is never regarded as the content of the quickened life; he is the agent of revelation who brings the content of truth to the spirit of men, and in consequence we have the mind of Christ. . . The Spirit is the quickening cause and the indwelling of Christ is the effect of the quickening. . . Christ is the objective ground of salvation, the Spirit is the effective cause of the new life in us.[9]

Others speak in the same vein: 'He is the revealer, not the revealed'.[10] John V. Taylor tells us: 'You cannot commune with the Holy Spirit because he is communion. . . You can never know the otherness of the Spirit, only the aliveness his presence brings, the inertness that comes from his absence. He acts anonymously and unnoticed.'[11] Hans Urs von Balthasar writes: 'This Spirit is breath, not form; that is why he only wished to penetrate us by his breath, and not to objectify himself for us; he does not wish to be seen, but he wishes to be in us the seeing eye of grace.'[12] J. V. Taylor makes the restriction on communing with the Holy Spirit apply to prayer: 'Prayer in the Spirit not to the Spirit is the pattern of the New Testament'.[13]

This difficulty about prayer to the Holy Spirit is an ancient one. In the fourth century Gregory of Nazianzen was confronted with the argument that the Holy Spirit was not divine because we did not pray to him. He found himself in a dilemma. He knew that the shape of the liturgy was prayer to the Father through the Son, in the Holy Spirit. He also knew that in early patristic times there is no evidence of prayers addressed to the Holy Spirit apart from a line in Origen. On the other hand Gregory had no doubt (and more important still the Church at large has no doubt) about the divinty of the Holy Spirit. Gregory's answer to the difficulty was not his finest moment, but it went along these lines: we do not pray to the Holy Spirit because it is he who enables us to pray, and so he would be praying to himself. Of course it was early days yet. The definition of Constantinople was still a few years away. The formula of the expanded Nicene Creed—*simul adoratur et conglorificatur*—underlined beyond any ambiguity the Holy Spirit's claim to our worship, our affection and our devotion. One of the Holy

Spirit's functions is to be a Guide: even the Russian Intourist can hardly insist that there by no conversation with their guides. The Christian instinct revolts against any attempt to forbid conversation with such a Guide as the Holy Spirit.

The footprints?

The cautionary note in some of these extracts has a certain validity, provided we do not push it too far to foster a 'benign neglect' of the Holy Spirit. Because we must see the face of the Spirit in Christ, other writers have sought for something distinctive about the 'footprints' of the Spirit. Some look for a clear differentiation of function, something which the Holy Spirit does which no other divine Person does: '(The Holy Spirit) acts and exists to act in a very different manner. . . (he) vitalises, renews, admonishes, warns, recalls, interprets, enlightens, guides, gives comfort, and strength.'[14]

However one of the most basic canons of trinitarian theology is that the operations of the Trinity *ad extra* are common to all three Persons. Widmar also overlooks this when he writes: 'If the Father is God outside us, remaining in Heaven in his absolute transcendence, if the Son is God with us partaking in our historicity the Holy Spirit is God in us.'[15] Moreover, this view seems to overlook the charter of divine indwelling in the last chapters of St John's Gospel, e.g. 'We will come to him and make our home with him' (Jn 14:23).

Earthing?

The search for the 'footprints' of the Spirit is a praiseworthy one. To be profitable it must be adequately 'earthed' and follow the direction of Christ, the Church and the sacraments. Montanists in the third century and subsequent movements of this kind spoke of an Age of the Spirit which they understood to transcend the achievements of Christ and offer a 'spiritual' religion superior to that of the institutional Church. This kind of thinking lies behind much of the literature on religions of authority and religions of the Spirit. Through it runs a failure to acknowledge the incarnational character of the Gospel. H. B. Swete expresses well something they overlook: 'There is to be no transference from the old life of obedience to Christ to the new Life in the Spirit; the latter is but the maturity of the former; the conditions are changed, but the continuity is unbroken. The Spirit does not come to supersede the Son but to glorify him.'[16] In other words the Mission of the Holy Spirit is not to set aside the work of the Son but to assure its success. The *Filioque* is most important in understanding the mission of the Holy Spirit—'Whom the Father will send in my name, he will teach you all things, and bring to your remembrance all that I have said to you... He will bear witness to me... He will glorify me for he will take what is mine and declare it to you' (Jn 14:26; 15:26; 16:14). Some Eastern orthodox theologians speak of the Incarnate Word as the 'Precursor' of the Holy Spirit. The expression is not a very happy one: it evokes memories of the original 'precursor' John the Baptist and his own summary of his position relative to our Lord—he must increase I must decrease. This does not express the proportions between the mission of the Son and the mission of the Holy Spirit.

Through the centuries people have misused the Holy Spirit's name to by-pass Christ, the Church and the sacraments, to establish a footloose and fancy free spirituality. As G. S. Hendry says: 'The presence of the Spirit does not supersede the presence of Christ... that is the spiritualist heresy that has plagued the Church repeatedly from the time of Montanus onward... the association of the Spirit with Christ prevents the dissolution of Christian faith into a general religiosity.'[17] Or as St Augustine puts it the Holy Spirit is not a break-away Spirit but the Spirit of unity.[18] Spiritual streakers of all kinds through the ages have claimed a particular blessing and inspiration of the Holy Spirit for their extravaganzas. It is true that spiritual streakers have run amok on other pretexts; yet the Holy Spirit has been a favourite stalking horse and a long history has caused a certain nervousness about a devotion to the Holy Spirit that is not sufficiently 'earthed'.

The Trinity

It is possible to quench devotion to the Holy Spirit in a sea of cautionary tales. Devotion to the Holy Spirit is not an optional extra if we are to develop our sense of God. How can we claim to have a sense of the Christian God—the Trinity—if the Holy Spirit is the great unmentionable? Without a sound trinitarian basis theology sags and with it spiritual theology and preaching. This clear in the Liberal German Protestant theology of the nineteenth century and its posterity today. In this line of thinking the Holy Spirit is an early casualty, and becomes a mere *modus loquendi*. An immediate consequence is the loss of a real notion of the supernatural. Inevitably the understanding of our relationship with God is blurred and the spiritual life is distorted.

Catholic theology has avoided these errors of base, but the follow-through has been disappointing. For a trinitarian religion the trinitarian side of our devotional life has been insufficiently developed. Despite the example of the liturgy and the opportunities it offers to ring the changes on various themes of Christian spirituality, we have succeeded in saying as little as is humanly possible about the Holy Spirit. Greater damage has been avoided because some of the slack is taken up by emphasis on other doctrines of our faith.

A Privileged Moment

In our own day Pope Paul VI has said 'we live in the Church at a privileged moment of the Holy Spirit' *(Evangelii Nuntiandi, n. 75)*. We must be neither pharisaical nor naive about this. We must not be pharisaical enough to believe that we are better instruments of the Holy Spirit than previous generations or that we offer less friction to his action. We must not be naive enough to imagine that the Holy Spirit is a soft option. If we want to understand the demands of a new Pentecost nothing is more sobering than a hard, clear look at the original Pentecost and its follow-through. Nor must we be naive enough to imagine that repeated shouting about the Holy Spirit is going to bring down the walls of Jericho outside of us and within us. The impact of devotion to the Holy Spirit—or any other devotion—on the world around us depends entirely on its effects on us.

A Sense of Loss

Today may be seen as a 'privileged moment of the Holy Spirit' because he is seen as overcoming a sense of loss that many experience. This sense of loss is felt particularly in the realm of prayer. Many feel caught between a loss of confidence in the older forms of devotion and prayer and inability to devise new forms. A younger generation is growing up which does not know the older forms and to the extent that it does is not especially attracted to them. Yet there is a manifest hunger for prayer among those who had given it up, those who have been freewheeling, and those who never knew it. One should not imagine that this had reached epidemic proportions, but it does exist. In a variety of ways people are asserting their conviction that 'not alone in bread doth man live'. For some this may simply involve taking their rat out of the race; for others it may be satisfied by climbing Everest, or sailing around the world, or walking around the countryside, or in 'good works'. In others, it is a specifically religious search, and some of our young people are being attracted to forms of religion and prayer—whether Eastern forms or Western sects—which make demands and offer challenges. Not all such assertions lead to Jesus Christ and the Holy Spirit. Even within the Church this is true. There is more than one movement inside the Church where dedication, and sacrifice, and single-mindedness are manifest, but which are very selective, and in consequence misdirected. A tiger in the tank does not guarantee the steering. Again, in all the flurry about people who have found prayer we should not forget those who never abandoned it, who all along have understood the heart of the older forms of prayer, and even *tempore non suspecto*, had a warm devotion to the Holy Spirit.

For many today the Holy Spirit is a new discovery. This is sometimes spoken of as the 'return of the Spirit'. The expression is unfortunate: the Holy Spirit has never been away. For some the Spirit is newly found, because too many of our people like the disciples of the Baptist in Ephesus of old hardly knew there was a Holy Spirit. With this discovery one can go to the opposite extreme of imagining that there is no one but the Holy Spirit. This leads to a monism of the Holy Spirit. The hunger for prayer of which we have spoken may drive us to accept anything that appears to fill and be impatient with the demands of a balanced diet.

The Demands of Devotion

If this privileged moment of the Holy Spirit is to be grasped fully then devotion to the Holy Spirit must attend to some norms which Pope Paul VI offers for devotion in general: 'One finds among the people particular expressions of the search for God and faith...these expressions were for a long time regarded as less pure and were sometimes despised, but today are almost everywhere being rediscovered *(Evangelii Nuntiandi, n. 48)*.

Elsewhere *(Marialis cultus)* Pope Paul indicates the true heart of some older forms of devotion. In *Evangelii Nuntiandi* he indicates how they may remain at the level of 'popular religiosity'. This has limitations: 'It is often subject to penetration by many distortions and even superstition. It frequently remains at the level of worship not involving a true acceptance of faith. It can lead to the creation of sects and endanger the true ecclesial community.' The Pope goes on to say that it can be a stepping stone. 'But if it is well oriented above all by a pedagogy of evangelisation, it is rich in values. It manifests a thirst for God which only the simple and the poor can know. It makes people capable of generosity and sacrifices even to the point of heroism when it is a question of manifesting belief. It involves an acute awareness of the profound attributes of God: fatherhood, providence, living and constant presence. It engenders interior attitudes rarely observed elsewhere —patience, the sense of the Cross in daily life, detachment, openness to others, devotion.' (n. 48).

Charismatic groups are often criticised because they manifest the less acceptable face of 'popular religiosity'. It can be argued too that some repeat a mistake made by 'devotees' in the past 'who without wholesome liturgical and pastoral criteria mix practices of piety and liturgical acts in hybrid celebrations... This creates the danger that the Lord's memorial rite, instead of being the culmination of the meeting of the Christian community becomes the occasion, as it were, for devotional practices' *(Marialis Cultus, no. 13)*. Contemporary movements are not exempt from the general law that exciting apostolates tend to attract excitable apostles. On the other hand it must be recognised that members often exhibit the good features of popular piety enumerated by Pope Paul. For some it can be a latching-on point—a beginning of the seek and knock operation which our Lord commends so highly. One can seek in the wrong places, and knock on the wrong doors, and keep on doing so. A 'pedagogy of evangelisation' is needed. In other words a catechesis.

Catechesis

This catechesis must ensure that rather more is said about the Holy Spirit. If we do not talk more about ehs Holy Spirit we tend to talk rather more about ourselves. It is important that the momentum of contemporary interest in the Holy Spirit does not peter out in *marginalia*. Our catechesis will depend on theological reflexion. H. Heine has said that 'men of action are nothing but the unconscious hodmen of the men of thought.'[19] Men at the front can be served in various ways by the backroom boys both in what they include and what they omit. Pope Paul VI has expressed the fear that many spiritual writings today do not sufficiently reflect the whole doctrine concerning the Holy Spirit *(Marialis Cultus, no. 27)*. What theology and catechesis have to say will vary according to circumstances in sophistication and articulation. St Cyril of Jerusalem told his people:

> The Father through the Son with the Holy Spirit is the giver of all grace; the gifts of the Father are none other than those of the Son and of the Holy Spirit; for there is one salvation, one power, one faith, one God the Father, one Lord his only begotten Son, one Holy Spirit the Comforter. And it is enough to know these things, but enquire not curiously into his nature or substance, for had it been written we would have spoken of it. What is not written let us not venture on. It is sufficient for our salvation to know that there is a Father, Son, and Holy Spirit.[20]

At first sight this may seem oversimple. However, if we look a little more closely it offers a ground plan for our catechesis which may be developed. The catecheses of the Fathers have a good deal to offer in

107

regard to the development of this ground plan, and perhaps especially in the manner in which they made their people 'mind-full' of the Holy Trinity. The Fathers in their catecheses inserted the mystery of the Trinity very firmly in the stream of consciousness of their people, and with it an awareness of the Holy Spirit and his work. Our efforts must work in the same direction. We shall find that many of our discoveries are, in reality, re-discoveries: others have been here before us. Here we cannot follow in detail the elements of their catecheses. They looked for and found the footprints of the Holy Spirit in Creation, the Old Testament, the Incarnation, the Church our Lady and the saints, in the life of grace and prayer, and Christian behaviour. They were open to the 'whole doctrine of the Holy Spirit'. Following in their wake we avoid seeing the Holy Spirit only where and how he interests us.

Devotion to the Holy Spirit

The past has much to contribute to our understanding of the doctrine of the Holy Spirit. It also has something to teach us about expressing our devotion to the Holy Spirit. There is, for instance a contrast between devotion to the Incarnate Word, and to the Holy Spirit. The contrast is not between devotion and no devotion—that there was devotion to the Incarnate Word and none to the Holy Spirit. The contrast is rather in the manner in which devotion expressed itself. From the Council of Ephesus onwards devotion to the Incarnate Word, and in consequence to our Lady and the saints, is a more obvious feature of the devotional life of the masses. Pope Paul points out that where liturgical spirit was declining these devotions favoured a certain external sentiment in piety (Marialis Cultus, no. 48). This can happen with any devotion which becomes detached from its roots. The emphasis on the humanity of our Saviour down the centuries was not simply because people followed the line of least resistance: nor was it because of lack of effort or shortage of inventiveness that the results were different in devotion to the Holy Spirit. The impact of Constantinople was no less in its way than that of Ephesis: the Church East and West had a strong and warm devotion to the Holy Spirit. The different of expression between devotion to the Holy Spirit and other devotions has to do with the nature of devotion itself.

Balance in Devotion

Devotion I take as simply another way of speaking about cleaving to God, or grasping God's extended hand gladly and gratefully. St Thomas Aquinas defines it in a workmanlike phrase: 'The prompt willingness to serve God'. Our Lord had already given the magisterial definition

'Thou shalt love the Lord your God with all your heart and all your soul and all your mind' (Mt 22:27). In other words, the love of God engages the whole person. From person to person this or that motor centre of devotion may be more in evidence. In some, this or that motor centre of devotion may be overloaded. Thus one may lay so much stress on the intellectual that God becomes a problem to be solved rather than a Person to be loved and served. Aquinas was quite right when he said that many an old lady knew more about God than many a great theologian. On the other hand one can overload the emotional, so that it is simply emotionalism, whose 'haunting vice is spiritual pride'.[21] With emotionalism the doctrinal input is so slight that the criterion is not how things are but how we feel.

Again certain theories and practices can eliminate a whole range of motor centres of devotion. The classic case is Iconoclasm. This was a kind of Docetism of the spiritual life. It was and remains a dangerous heresy. It was not only a mistake about what makes man tick, but a serious misunderstanding of the Incarnation. It wished to mute a whole range of motor centres which help a man to find his God. It surfaces from time to time in the history of the Church, in the quest for purer and more abstract religious forms. Various schools of 'pure love' have been the grandchildren of the Iconoclasts. Such attempts to suppress an important and valid exercise of our emotions usually produce a counter movement in which humanity re-asserts itself. Pietism is a case in point. Sometimes such movements become suspicious of theological subtleties: they feel in their bones that such subtleties have led to wrong conclusions, and they tend to distrust any doctrinal input. This leaves them with the 'feel in their bones', and we are back to emotionalism.

The Church's reaction to Iconoclasm has been to assert the value of the audio-visual in religion: we are not disembodied spirits. God is given to us and we must grasp him through the full range of faculties with which we are endowed and in and through the Incarnation.

The consequences for devotion have been noted by medieval theologians. St Thomas Aquinas' words are, perhaps, the best known, but the substance is commonplace in earlier times:

Matters concerning the Godhead are in themselves the strongest incentive to love, and consequently to devotion because God is supremely lovable, yet such is the weakness of the human mind that it needs a guiding hand, not only to the knowledge but also to the love of divine things by means of certain sensible objects known to us. Chief among these is the humanity of Christ...so those things which pertain to the humanity of Christ, are the chief incentive to devotion though devotion itself is principally concerned with those that belong to divinity.[22]

or again:

Divine realities can only be manifested to men under sensible images: these images move the soul the more they are communicated not only in words but in so far as they are offered to the senses.[23]

The theology of the Holy Spirit offers few concessions to the senses, and this makes specific devotions to the Holy Spirit less easy to devise. The Incarnation with its history: the birth, the actions, the words, the whole life and death and resurrection affect all the motor centres of devotion. Christian prayer and reflection over the centuries has developed many different devotions accenting this or that aspect of the Incarnation. In the nature of things this has not been so easy for the Holy Spirit. Those who have not realised this have often gone off on tangents, that in the long run hinder rather than help devotion to the Holy Spirit. On the other hand the history of devotion also bears witness to the firm, warm and constant devotion of the Church to the Holy Spirit expressed in sober, patient forms.

Specific devotions and prayers apart, the Holy Spirit is there in all our prayer. Pope Pius XII has expressed this well:

These traditional exercises [i.e. the traditional popular devotions] cannot but be inspired and influenced by the Holy Ghost; in their various ways they tend to raise up the soul to God, to purify it from sin, and urge it to the pursuit of virtue, and give it a love for true piety; they accustom us to meditating on the eternal truths and dispose us to contemplate the mysteries of the divinity and humanity of Christ.[24]

The Holy Spirit is present in these exercises: it needs only a turn of the mind to acknowledge that presence and his work. Devotion to the Holy Spirit is seen by many as an apprenticeship to prayer: it should be open to the whole range of prayer.

I have said that devotion to the Holy Spirit is not an optional extra: without him the full story is not told. Because he is one of the divine Three, he is, in the fine expression of Richard of St Victor 'condilectus' —co-beloved in the Trinity itself, and among those who love the Trinity. Today when many take a socio-political view of many spiritual realities, from Christ, through the Church, to the sense of life, the Holy Spirit and his mission remind us of the true balance. Awareness of the Holy Spirit allows us to see beyond mere philanthropy, fellow-feeling and humanism. It urges us to recognise this *Dulcis Hospes Animae* and try to be worthy of this Guest.

NOTES

1. H. Berkhof, *The Doctrine of the Holy Spirit*, pp. 115, 128 n. 6.
2. 'The Doctrine of the Spirit and the Task of a Theology of Nature', in *Theology*, January 1972.
3. Cf. H. M. B. Reid, *The Holy Spirit and the Mystics*, pp. 15f.
4. *Oratio Catechetica*, c. 2.
5. Cited in H. Watkins-Jones, *The Holy Spirit in the Medieval Church*, p. 172.
6. *De Trinitate*, xv. 39.
7. *De Trinitate*, iv. 20.
8. See Fison, *The Blessing of the Spirit*, p. 176; V. Lossky, *The Mystical Theology of the Eastern Church*, p. 168.
9. L. S. Thornton, *The Incarnate Lord*, p. 323, cited (and also criticised) by A. W. Wainwright, *The Trinity in the New Testament*, p. 219.
10. O. C. Quick, *Doctrines of the Creed*, p. 300.
11. *The Go-Between God: The Holy Spirit and the Christian Mission*, p. 43.
12. 'L'Esprit inconnu au dela du Verbe' in *Lumiere et Vie*, n. 67, p. 121.
13. *The Go-Between God: The Holy Spirit and the Christian Mission*, p. 44.
14. C. W. Lowry, *The Trinity and Christian Devotion*, p. 71.
15. 'Saint Esprit et theologie trinitaire' in F. J. Leenhardt et al., *Le Saint Esprit*, p. 116.
16. H. B. Swete, *Studies in the Teaching of our Lord*, p. 151.
17. *The Holy Spirit in Christian Theology*, p. 41.
18. *Sermo* 269: Pl 38 1236.
19. *Religion and Philosophy in Germany*, p. 106.
20. *Catechetical Lectures*, 16. 24.
21. H. M. B. Reid, *The Holy Spirit and the Mystics*, p. 51.
22. *Summa Theologiae*, II-II, q. 82, art. 3 ad 3.
23. *Summa Theologiae*, I-II, q. 99, art. 3 ad 3.
24. *Mediator Dei*, n. 187.

Redemption

TORAH AND *MISHPAT* – A LIGHT TO THE PEOPLES

Anthony Phillips

There can be little doubt that Israel regarded the Babylonian conquest and her subsequent exile in a heathen land as the most cataclysmic event in her history. The destruction of the temple, the captivity of the king and leading citizens and the absorption of her land into the Babylonian empire seem to mark her end as a distinct people, the people of Yahweh. Could there be any future?

But one element in Israel's life was not destroyed, her law, though paradoxically Israel's theologians considered that its breach had led to her apparent hopeless situation. For it was not Babylonian military prowess which had brought this about, but Yahweh himself who could no longer tolerate Israel's disobedience. But ironically if there was to be any future, that future depended on Israel continuing to express faith in Yahweh, and the only sure vehicle for that faith was his law.

In the aftermath of the disaster of 586 the Deuteronomists produced what was on the face of it one of the most remarkable testimonies to faith ever written. By modelling the book of Deuteronomy on the political suzerainty treaty form they clearly indicated that they understood the continuation of the covenant relationship with Yahweh to be determined by Israel's obedience to the stipulations he had laid upon her. Whether earlier generations had interpreted Israel's relationship with Yahweh in the same way need not concern us.[1] But for the Deuteronomists Israel's election contained within it the threat of rejection if she failed to keep the covenant law laid upon her by her suzerain, Yahweh. Yet though they understood that threat to have been implemented by the events of 586, the Deuteronomists none the less produced their great theological work, Deuteronomy–2 Kings. Their hope, apparently illogical, was that despite all that had occurred, Yahweh might yet once more exercise his grace, that there might be another entry into the promised land.

The event which apparently prompted the Deuteronomists to articulate their hope was the release of King Jehoiachin from prison in 561. Undoubtedly this caused enormous excitement throughout Judaism both in Palestine and Babylon. Could this be the prelude to yet another mighty act of Yahweh? For those who had eyes to see, was he even now preparing to deliver his people? So in spite of their own theological position, the Deuteronomists were prepared to recognise that Yahweh could not let his people go. This was their testimony of faith.

But if there was to be a future, that future could only be built on Yahweh's *torah*. Hence the Deuteronomists reiterate the importance of absolute obedience to the covenant law, which they set out in every detail. If ever again Israel is given the chance to cross the Jordan she will know what she has to do in order to ensure that she should not once more be cursed for her failure. It is thus no accident that it is the Deuteronomists who reinterpret the word *torah* from its earlier use as a specific direction following a particular question to designate the whole corpus of the law. It therefore comes to stand for the complete expression of the will of Yahweh. So, as Barnabas Lindars has indicated, the usual translation 'the book of the law' would be better rendered 'the book of divine instruction'.[2] This development was probably the work of the scribal school now widely thought to have been behind Deuteronomy[3] for it is in the wisdom literature that *torah* is used quite generally of the teaching of the wise rather than in the priestly sense as an answer to a query. In any event, for the Deuteronomists the individual laws are intended as a comprehensive list to deal with every situation which Israel may face in the promised land, and thus enable her at all times to fulfill Yahweh's will. Consequently the *torah* must on no account be varied either by addition or subtraction (Dt 4:2: 12:32). This is not an uncommon element in ancient Near Eastern law codes as the conclusion of the Babylonian codes of Lipit Ishtar[4] and Hammurabi[5] indicate. But it may at first seem surprising that the Deuteronomists considered their code complete when it makes no reference to the civil law provisions which are so important in the Book of the Covenant. But as I have pointed out in my commentary on Deuteronomy,[6] the reason for this was that such provisions were not understood as part of the covenant law on which Israel's continued election depended, but rather as domestic issues to be settled between the parties through the payment of damages. The Deuteronomic law is not concerned with the protection of property but with establishing that society which reflects Yahweh's will. Hence its stress on sole allegiance to him and the exercise of charity to those in need. For it was by an act of charity, the exercise of his grace, that Yahweh had chosen Israel and brought her to the promised land, and might yet do so again.

It is then on the strength of the history of Yahweh's dealings with his people that the Deuteronomists appeal to their contemporaries to remain faithful. For if Yahweh is to continue to exercise his grace towards Israel, there must still be a people whom he can deliver. For the Deuteronomists, then, despite judgment having been carried out under the law, that law must not be considered obsolete. For it is with those who still acknowledge its validity that Yahweh can do, if he so wills, his further mighty work. In other words, though Israel's future depends on the initiative of Yahweh, Yahweh is himself dependent on there being a faithful people on whom he can lavish his illogical generosity (comp. Hos 11:8-9), and who will then once more be able to practise his *torah* in their own land and so entirely fufill his will. Then they will enjoy unparalleled prosperity as they luxuriate in the rich ordering of life which obedience to *torah* always brings. This was the vision which the Deuteronomists offered their generation.

The Deuteronomists produced their work sometime between the release of Jehoiachin from prison in 561 and 540, for they show no awareness of the threat to Babylon from the rise of Cyrus, nor make any mention of the return from exile in 538. Whether they wrote in Babylon or Palestine remains uncertain. Their work was shortly followed by the prophecies of Deutero-Isaiah.

This unknown prophet of the exile, like the Deuteronomists, proclaimed a message of hope against a background of total failure. No attempt is made to gloss over Israel's sin which had brought her to her present position. But the emphasis of Deutero-Isaiah's prophecy and the basis for his hope is that Yahweh who is both lord of creation and lord of history (e.g. Is 51:9-11) is still in control, though the responsibility for Israel's future rests entirely on the exiles.

Deutero-Isaiah was not the first prophet to proclaim a return from exile. Ezekiel had done so many years before. But the generation to whom Ezekiel had preached was already dead, and there still seemed to be no end to Israel's sojourn in Babylon. The only sensible conclusion must be to accept that Yahweh's judgment had been final, as the Deuteronomic covenant theology implied (though the Deuteronomists hoped that this was not so), and identify with foreign and apparently victorious gods. Against such a background Deutero-Isaiah announces that even now Yahweh is breaking in to perform his new mighty act. Israel's redemption was not merely imminent but accomplished (Is 48:20). His message is then one of realised eschatology. It is no accident that this all-conquering Persian prince has appeared in the east, but part of the divine plan. Israel's punishment is over and the whole world will witness her triumphant procession across a transformed environment back to her own land (Is 40:1-11). And this new exodus in which water will be abundantly available to the chosen people (Is 43:19-21) will be no secret

114

flight (Is 52:12), but will take place in full sight of the nations. It may have looked as if Yahweh had abandoned his people, but there had in fact been no bill of divorce (Is 50:1). But unlike the Deuteronomists who make no attempt to reassess Yahweh's relationship with his people, but still see Israel as subject to the threat of total rejection, Deutero-Isaiah assures the exiles that this relationship will be for all time. In the future nothing will be able to sever Yahweh's covenant with his people for in the new exodus from Babylon, unlike its predecessor from Egypt, no obligations will be laid on them. Deutero-Isaiah arrives at this 'new covenant' theology of sheer grace (comp. Jer 31) — a theology also to be found in Ezekiel and the Priestly Work — by omitting any reference to the Sinai covenant (Exod 19ff).[7] Instead he concentrates on Israel's three ancient covenant traditions — all covenants of promise without obligation: the covenants with Noah (Gen 8:21-2), Abraham (Gen 17), and David (2 Sam 7). Thus the covenant with Abraham is proclaimed as still in force (Is 51:2-3), the covenant with Noah reiterated (Is 54:9-10), and the covenant with David reapplied to the nation (Is 55:3). The only element of hesitation in the prophet's triumphant message is whether the exiles will have sufficient faith to recognise in the events now engulfing them the hand of Yahweh who wills that they should continue to be his people and he their God. Their future is assured for ever, if only they will appropriate what is at present at hand.

But is it only in the abandonment of the Deuteronomic threat theology that Deutero-Isaiah differs from the Deuteronomists? Could it also be said that his attitude to the foreign nations marks a complete reversal of Deuteronomic concern? Certainly this view was once generally accepted. Deutero-Isaiah was seen as charging the chosen people, now specifically designated as 'a light to the nations' (Is 42:6; 49:6), with an active mission to the world. Having been individually elected to receive Yahweh's revelation, they are now to set about sharing it with all nations. But recent studies of Deutero-Isaiah by de Boer,[8] Snaith[9] and Martin-Achard[10] have challenged such an interpretation. Far from Deutero-Isaiah being the apostle of missionary zeal, his prophecies have been understood as narrowly nationalistic and particularist. So de Boer argues that Deutero-Isaiah's 'only purpose is to proclaim deliverance for the Judean people'[11] an assessment which both Snaith and, more judiciously, Martin-Achard support. So the latter writes: 'The chief concern of the prophet of the Exile is not the salvation of the Gentiles but the liberation of his own people and its triumphant return to Jerusalem; the heathen are scarcely more than an instrument in the hands of Israel's God.'[12] The result of such an interpretation is that Deutero-Isaiah is held responsible for the allegedly narrow and exclusive attitude of

115

post-exilic Judaism, and any tension between his prophecy and the work of Nehemiah and Ezra is removed. But in my view this interpretation of Deutero-Isaiah's work does as much violence to his prophecy as the interpretation it rightly overthrows.[13] While Deutero-Isaiah nowhere bids Israel actually to go out in mission to the foreign nations, he is none the less positively concerned about their relationship with Yahweh. While he rejoices over Yahweh's unexpected deliverance of Israel, he by no means sees this in narrow nationalistic terms, but as having definite repercussions on the nations who are thereby brought to acknowledge Yahweh as the one sovereign God. As a result, Yahweh's *torah* and *mishpat* now become of universal significance and the means whereby world order can be achieved.

The Deuteronomic attitude to foreign nations is clear enough. In the Deuteronomists' opinion Israel's failure to destroy the Canaanites on first entry into the land had led to her subsequent apostasy, and so to Yahweh's judgment for her unfaithfulness. Consequently the Deuteronomists urge that were the Jordan ever to be crossed for a second time, then this time the indigenous population must be utterly exterminated. Of course one has only to compare the prophecy of Hosea with Deuteronomic theology to recognise that this Deuteronomic assessment is decidely one-sided. In fact in every department of her life and not least in her understanding of her God, Israel's debt to Canaan was immense. But for the Deuteronomists writing in the aftermath of the Babylonian conquest and exile, it was Canaanite religious practice which had polluted the pure Yahwistic faith and led to Israel's renunciation by her God. Hence the Deuteronomists concentrate on ensuring the isolation of Israelite religion from all Canaanite customs and practices. (Dt 14; 18:9-14; 21:22-23; 22:5; 23:17-18). Thus while under earlier regulations marriages with Canaanite women had been frowned upon (Ex 34:16), now they are totally banned with both men and women (Dt 7:3; Josh 23:12; Judg 3:6). The Deuteronomists see Israel as a religious ghetto in faithful obedience to Yahweh revelling in the richness of the land which he wills to give her. They know that they are better off than any of the other nations both in their God's concern for them and the nature of his will, his *torah* (Dt 4:7-8), and are content to leave the other nations to their inferior gods. Their conversion is thus never contemplated. But within Israel—that is the whole territory of the promised land—Yahweh is to enjoy his people's exclusive worship. What happened outside is no concern of theirs. In this respect, as in my view in their covenant threat theology, the Deuteronomists were merely re-iterating the recognised pre-exilic position. While Yahweh is seen as having power to do with the nations as he likes, both in using them as

116

his agent and also inflicting judgment upon them, it is only with Israel that he has entered into a specific relationship and only from her that he expects unwavering allegiance (Amos 3:2).

The basis for the view that Deutero-Isaiah specifically charged Israel with a mission to the world lies in the fact that he is the first Old Testament theologian explicitly to articulate the doctrine of monotheism. that is, that there is only one God (Is 41:4; 43:10-13; 44:6-8; 45:5-6, 14, 18, 22; 46:9; 48:12). Earlier Israel had, of course, worshipped only one God, but had freely acknowledged the existence of other gods with whom she was forbidden to have any dealings. This milestone in the development of Israel's religious understanding was no doubt prompted by finding that in Babylon the same things were being claimed for Marduk as for Yahweh. The exponents of the missionary view of Deutero-Isaiah's ministry then argue that the immediate effect of the declaration of monotheism was to bring the other nations which could hitherto be comfortably ignored into a definite relationship with Yahweh, for as the only God he must have been responsible for their creation. This accounts for the new world view of Deutero-Isaiah. Logically this must be the case. If there is only one God, the creator of all, then all must be of intimate concern to him. The Deuteronomic ghetto theology cannot be maintained. But it does not necessarily follow from this that the only way in which Yahweh can express his concern is by charging Israel with an active mission to the nation. They can equally well get to know Yahweh and his will by coming themselves to Israel to be taught by her.

The missionary view of Deutero-Isaiah's prophecy is based on four key texts Is 42:1-4; 49:1-6; 51:4-5 and 55:3-5. In Is 42:1-4, the first of the so-called servant songs (Is 42:1-4[9]; 49:1-6[13]; 50:4-9[11]; 52:13—53:12), Yahweh designates his chosen servant through whom he wills that his *mishpat* shall be brought forth to the nations. A final note adds that even those most distant places, the coastlands or isles (verse 4) await Yahweh's *torah*. In this task the servant strengthened by Yahweh's spirit is assured of success, even when others might have been discouraged. The hint that this discouragement will consist of severe personal suffering is confirmed in the later songs.

But before we go any further we must ask who is this servant? Despite the multitude of words which have been written on this subject[14] there can to my mind be no doubt who has formed Deutero-Isaiah's model. For as we would expect in a work depicting a second exodus, it can only be Moses for he alone of all Israel's heroes was specifically said to have suffered vicariously at Yahweh's behest.[15] The first intimation of this occurs in the account in Exodus of the incident of the golden calf

(Ex 32:32), in my view the work of the JE redactor,[16] where Moses is described as offering to atone for Isarel's sin. It is on this incident that the Deuteronomists have built. For them Yahweh takes the initiative and specifically refuses to allow Moses to enter the promised land (Dt 1:37; 3:26-28; 4:21). Instead he is instructed to look across the Jordan at the full extent of that land, and so to take possession of it on Israel's behalf, for this was the recognised legal way by which the conveyance of land was effected (comp. Gen 13:14-17).[17] But although himself innocent of any offence, Moses must die in Transjordan for Israel's rebellion in the desert. This theological assessment was too much for the Priestly theologians who reinterpreted Yahweh's refusal to allow Moses entry into the promised land as due to actual sin on his part (Num 20:12; Dt 32:51).[18] But it is this explicit example of vicarious suffering, the work of the Deuteronomists, who incidentally continually describe Moses as 'the servant of God', which has directly influenced Deutero-Isaiah.

But establishing the model for the suffering servant does not mean that we have discovered that servant's identity. Who is to be the new Moses of the new exodus? From Is 49:3 the answer would seem to be Israel,[19] but Is 49:6 makes it plain that this cannot be all Israel. Rather the servant must be that righteous remnant of Israel who remain faithful to Yahweh and by accepting Deutero-Isaiah's message secure the future of all Israel. It is those individuals who in the face of the apparent inactivity of Yahweh are still prepared to acknowledge and trust him. It seems then to me that we are to see in the dying generation of the faithful exiles a direct parallel to Moses who like them had to die in a heathen land beyond the Jordan in order that his people might enter the promised land. Their faithfulness in suffering would ultimately have world-wide significance. The servant will not have laboured in vain: he need not be discouraged.

According to Is 42:1-4 the servant's task is to bring forth, that is manifest, *mishpat* among the nations. This word is usually rendered in English by judgement or justice. But neither term adequately expresses its meaning. In Ex 21:1 the plural *mishpatim* is used collectively of the various injunctions of the Book of the Covenant (Ex 20:20–23:33). Originally *mishpatim* here referred only to the specific decisions on criminal and civil cases, for the laws on humaneness and righteousness (Ex 22:20-26; 23:1-9) are a later addition.[20] Thus the *mishpatim* represented actual court rulings which also acted as precedents for the future. But these precedents did, of course, directly reflect the will of Yahweh who was regarded as the author of all such decision. Consequently further injunctions which could not be enforced in the courts, the laws of humaneness and righteousness, could be subsumed under the title *mishpatim* as they too were seen to reflect the divine will. Collectively then *mishpat* could be understood as indicating the kind of conduct which Yahweh wanted his people to put into effect in their lives. Thus Jeremiah understands *mishpat* as a synonum for the way (*derek*) in which Yahweh wishes Israel to walk (5:4f). It is then in this sense of applied law, that is applying Yahweh's will to the whole stratum of life, that *mishpat* is to be understood in Is 42:1-4. It is this that the servant is to establish among the nations so that the whole world lives the kind of life that Yahweh wills. It comes then as no surprise to find both in Is 42:4 and the very similar passage Is 51:4 *mishpat* used in parallel with *torah* in its novel Deuteronomic sense of divine instruction, that is the collective expression of the will of Yahweh. Further investigation indicates that it is only in this Deuteronomic sense that *torah* is used by Deutero-Isaiah (Is 42:21, 24; 51:7). As in the case of the suffering servant, we here find another instance of direct Deuteronomic influence on Deutero-Isaiah.

The servant's task then is to bring forth *mishpat* to the nations. But in effecting this, he is not left unaided. At his call, Yahweh endows him with his spirit. The same gift of the spirit occurs in Is 11:2 where the Messianic king is similarly equipped in order that he might perform his task of establishing justice. Indeed it is possible that as in Is 53:3 promises concerning the Davidic monarch have again been reapplied to faithful Israel. For there can be no doubt that for Deutero-Isaiah the prophecy of Is 11 will be fulfilled not by a restoration of the Davidic line and the reign of an ideal king, but rather by the work of the servant in establishing *mishpat* among the nations. It was this universalistic aspect of the servant's mission that a later editor of Isaiah felt obliged to add to the original, and in my view Isaianic Messianic prophecy (Is 11:10).

But curiously the servant is to achieve his task without crying or lifting up his voice. This would seem to rule out a mission to the nations to proclaim Yahweh's will such as Amos' mission to the northern kingdom. But perhaps in view of Is 11 we should see here a reference to the royal proclamation of the law following the king's coronation. In verse 3 we learn that the exercise of *mishpat* can only bring life even in apparently hopeless situations (comp. Is 40:6-8). Finally the song hints that the servant will fulfil his commission solely by his persistent endurance in the face of personal adversity. Until then the far off places must wait for Yahweh's *torah*.

In what is usually regarded as an addition to the first song, Is 42:6 designates the servant as *berit 'am* ('convenant of the people') and *'or goyim'* ('a light to the nations'). Both phrase occur again in Is 49.

The precise meaning of *berit 'am* is very uncertain. Indeed the phrase 'give as a *berit*' occurs nowhere else in the Old Testament. For this reason the New English Bible here rejects the normal translation of *berit* as 'covenant' and follows the suggestion originally made by Torczyner that *berit* should here be derived from a root *brr* meaning 'give light', 'shine'.[21] Lk 2:32 ('a light for revelation to the Gentiles, and for glory to thy people Israel') lends some support to this suggestion. But it is perhaps better to understand *berit* in its usual sense as derived from *brh* 'bind together', than look for a new word found nowhere else in the Old Testament. The servant then can be understood as the one who binds up. *'am* (people) is in the singular and should as is normal in Deutero-Isaiah be interpreted as such and here understood as referring to Israel.[22] It is true that in two instances, the preceding verse Is 42:5 and Is 40:7 *'am* singular is to be taken in a plural sense and understood as referring to the nations at large. But in view of the parallel passage in Is 49, it is clear that the servant's task is first to bind up scattered Israel (Is 49:8) and thereby to act as a light to the nations (Is 49:6). This means that the action which Is 42:7 goes on to describe, giving sight to the blind and releasing the prisoners, does not, as a number of commentators have argued, refer to the nations. For the use of the blind elsewhere in Is 42 and the parallel passage in Is 49:9 indicate that in Is 42:7 too reference is being made to the exiles. Thus the servant's role as a light to the nations is intimately connected with Israel's forthcoming deliverance from Babylon. It is through this miraculous event that the servant will be able to bring the nations into relationship with Yahweh. But while the initiative for the deliverance lies with Yahweh, whether or not he can do so is entirely dependent on the servant's faithfulness.

It is this faithfulness that is in doubt in the second servant song, Is 49:1-6, significantly addressed to the most distant nations. In the face of the futility of his endeavours, the servant is tempted to give up. This results in Yahweh not only confirming the servant's taks to restore Israel, but also extending the scope of his commission to involve the salvation of the whole world (Is 49:6). The following verse indicates how that salvation is to be effected. It will occur as the direct consequence of Yahweh's deliverance of his people (Is 49:7). In the face of such a miraculous turn of events the nations leaders will come and prostrate themselves before Israel in Zion. It is through Yahweh's glorification of the once despised people that Israel will assume a commanding role among the nations and become the hub of the whole world (Is 55:5). Just as once David through his military prowess became a leader among nations (Ps 18:43-45) so now Israel through Yahweh's grace will inherit the role of David (Is 55:4-5). For the following the totally unexpected vindication of Israel, the survivors of the nations will have no alternative but to acknowledge that Yahweh alone is God (Is 45:20-25) and therefore to submit to his authority. The servant will then through divine grace be able to fulfil his commission of being a light to the nations without himself undertaking a mission to the world, but through the world coming to the servant. He will then be able to bring the nations into a relationship with Yahweh and illuminate to them his divine will. For it must not be forgotten that the purpose of his commission was that Yahweh's salvation should no longer be limited to Israel but stretch to the end of the earth. It is for this that the most distant places wait (Is 42:4). And the way whereby the servant is to achieve this task is through revealing to the nations Yahweh's *torah* and *mishpat* which they will now accept and practise. That this is Yahweh's end purpose is confirmed from Is 51:4-5 where *torah* and *mishpat* are themselves seen as *'or 'amim*, a light to the peoples, here specifically in the plural, who expectantly wait for Yahweh's rule. But again it is stressed that the ultimate initiative for bringing Yahweh's salvation to the farthest places does not lie with Israel, but with Yahweh himself. So he assures his people that the covenant with Abraham (comp Is 41:8) is still in force, and despite all appearances to the contrary Israel's land will be restored to the pre-fall paradisal state (Is 51:1-3). Here we appear to have another echo of Is 11 which also pictures a return to paradise as wild and domestic animals lie down together in peace and children play in safety by snakes' nests. But more—Is 51 goes on to describe how the ancient hope that Abraham will be the father of all peoples (Gen 12:3) is now to be fulfilled through the dissemination of Yahweh's *torah* and *mishpat* even to the farthest places. As a result they too must enjoy the paradisal state for Gen 12:3 is the Yahwist's answer to the curse of Babel when all the nations of the world became scattered from Yahweh's presence (Gen 11). It is the servant's task to secure the reversal of that curse and a return to the original paradisal state where men dwelt together in unity and peace. For Yahweh who began the history of salvation in the call of Abraham is still in control of that history, and when history ends, symbolised in the apocalyptic language of the destruction of the heavens and the earth, his salvation will still endure (Is 51:6).

What then can we say of the motive behind Deutero-Isaiah's prophecy? Martin-Achard observes 'that actually about two-thirds of Deutero-Isaiah's utterances are devoted to persuading his contemporaries that the hour of Israel's liberation and its return to the Holy Land had come. . . The monotheistic and universalistic elements that we find in Isaiah xl-lv are not the essence of the prophet's message; their function is to corroborate his proclmation that the People are Yahweh will be comforted'[24] (Is 42:10ff; 43:7; 45:23; 49:26). But he fails to appreciate that the motive behind the whole work is Deutero-Isaiah's appreciation that it is not merely Israel's fate that is at issue but Yahweh's too. Without a community who in the face of all the evidence to the contrary will remain faithful, Yahwism is doomed. Israel's eventual restoration may be due to another divine act of grace, but that restoration is dependent on there being a faithful remnant to restore. Hence for all the assurances which Deutero-Isaiah lavishes on his hearers, he himself remains anxious about the outcome. It is by no means assured, and Yahweh himself is powerless to assure it. If the exiles as a whole apostatise, there will be no future. And Deutero-Isaiah knows that the cards are stacked against Yahweh. Ezekiel's prophecy had not been fulfilled; many of those to whom he preached were dead. Deliverance may be at hand; Cyrus may even now be coming from the east. But until that deliverance is recognised as a fact, then the faithful remnant must continue to fulfil their role through dogged endurance. There is no other way. A destiny far beyond the exiles' wildest dreams awaits them—far more than a mere Deuteronomic re-entry into the promised land—but that destiny can only be achieved through the passive acceptance of their present suffering which makes them utterly repugnant to the nations. This is the servant's task and Deutero-Isaiah drives it home in the third and fourth servant songs (Is 50:4-9; 52:13—53:12). But if the faithful persevere they will be vindicated and through their vindication bring salvation to the world. Their suffering will therefore be seen to have been on behalf of even those nations who had hitherto despised them.

But what will be the status of the foreign nations following Israel's vindication? Deutero-Isaiah does, of course, exult over the forthcoming destruction of Israel's enemies and the nations' humiliation before her (Is 49:26). But Israel's vindication can only be publicly manifested through the defeat of her enemies, and Yahweh's salvation only reach the farthest places in so far as those places accept his authority. This will inevitably mean humiliation as the nations discover that their whole future blessing depends on Israel and her God (Is 45:14). Further, in his appeal to the suffering faithful, it was inevitable that Deutero-Isaiah should emphasise the reversal of fortunes which Yahweh's act of deliverance would bring. Those who had enslaved Israel would themselves act as slaves in helping in her own restoration (Is 49:22-23). But this does not mean that the nations were to be kept in a permanent state of slavery. While they were to continue to be dependent on Israel, for from the call of Abraham she had been Yahweh's chosen means of enlightenment to the world, they too are to enjoy his blessing. Nor is there any hint in Deutero-Isaiah of their political absorption into Israel. They remain independent but united to Israel through their acknowledgement of the one and only God. While Deutero-Isaiah's prophecy is naturally much more concerned with the immediate issue—the preservation of a faithful remnant through whom Yahweh can redeem the world—that world's redemption remains his ultimate aim (Is 45:20-25). For without it there could be no return to Eden. And that will only come about through the universal acknowledgement of Yahweh's *torah* and *mishpat*. It is as mediator of the law that Israel acquires her title 'a light to the nations', but it is the law itself that constitutes that light.

The high hopes of Deutero-Isaiah did not materialise following the return from exile, but in the work called Trito-Isaiah those hopes are kept alive. Whether the author wrote before or after the rebuilding of the temple remains uncertain. Central to his message lies Yahweh's *torah* and *mishpat*. Thus at its very opening Trito-Isaiah dramatically extends Deutero-Isaiah's renunciation of Deuteronomic theology in respect of the nations. While Is 56:1 still looks forward to that miracle through which Yahweh's salvation will come and a new age dawn, Is 56:3ff, in complete contradiction to Deut 23:2-9, ordains that both a foreigner and a eunuch are to be admitted to the worshipping community of Israel provided they keep the law. As in other post-exilic material, sabbath observance is emphasised, being one of the clear outward distinguishing marks of membership of Judaism. The other, circumcision, may well be alluded to in the reference to 'my covenant', since the Priestly theologians reinterpreted circumcision as the specific sign of the covenant and transferred it to the eigth day after birth (Gen 17).[25] But the importance of Is 56 is that Judaism is open to any who wish to enter: previous race is to be no bar. All that is required is that those who seek membership of the elect community should obey the *torah*. Nor are these converts to Judaism to be treated in any way as second class citizens. They have absolute right of entry to the temple and their sacrifices are entirely acceptable to Yahweh. They act as a sign of the coming new age.

Is 60—61 pictures that new age, though this is now realised not in some specific historical event, but rather as a miraculous change in Israel's fortunes. Since the return from exile had taken place, there was now no 'historical' deliverance to look forward to. None the less this miraculous change of fortune continued to be seen in terms of a return of the exiles, for in fact following Cyrus' edict very few Jews had gone back to Palestine. In addition the foreigners who had destroyed the Judean cities would rebuild them and their kings who had enslaved Israel minister to her. The climax comes in Is 61 which is directly modelled on Is 42. So the prophet speaks as the Messianic prince of Is 11 to whom Yahweh had given his spirit. Part of his commission is to bind up the broken-hearted, a reference to the restoration of life in Is 42:3. As in Is 42:7 the captive exiles are to be released and Israel restored to her former glory. The prophecy than dramatically describes Israel as priest nation to the world. Just as in pre-exilic Israel the laity did all they manual work and supplied the non-property owning clergy with the livelihood, so the foreign nations will serve Israel who will eat their wealth and glory in their riches—riches brought about by the nations now being in communion with Yahweh. But Is 61:5 must not be interpreted in narrow nationalistic terms as if all Israel was to do was to enjoy herself at the expense of the now servile nations. She has a particular responsibility to be their priest, the chief of whose duties was, of course, to teach *torah* (Dt 33:10). Is 61:5-7 thus pictures the fulfilment of the servant's commission in Is 42:1-4 with Israel establishing throughout the world the practice of the complete will of Yahweh, his *mishpat*. That the servile role of the nations is not to be taken literally in Is 61:5-7 is confirmed by Is 62:8-9 and 65:21-22 where restored Israel is shown as now being able to enjoy the fruits of her own agricultural and building work. The importance of the vision of Is 61:5-7 is that it confirms that in the new age Israel is not destined for political superiority to be maintained by force of arms, but rather is to be the servant of the servants of Yahweh maintaining world peace through the dissemination of his *torah* and *mishpat*. Israel, now no longer a nation but a worshipping community, is thus at last able to fulfil her pre-conquest designated role as a kingdom of priests (Ex 19:6)—a role which her long period of nationhood had paradoxically prevented her from realising.

Zech 8:20-23 also takes up the theme of Israel as the priest nation, though there it is applied individually to each Jew who himself is to be a priest to the world. But as in Deutero-Isaiah it is because of what God has done for Israel that the foreign nations will come to her and not through any achievement on her part. Both in restoring Israel and willing to dwell in her midst in the rebuilt temple, Yahweh declares his nature to the nations of the world who now, through Israel, have the means of enjoying his grace. So a new age of salvation dawns, and that salvation is for the whole world. For it is God's world, and all men part of his creation and so eligible for membership of his elect community which is mankind itself.

The final chapter of Trito-Isaiah confirms that it will not be through Israel's missionary endeavour that the farthest lands will hear of Yahweh's *torah* and *mishpat*. Building on Is 45:20-25 where the survivors of the nations are brought to acknowledge Yahweh as the only God, Trito-Isaiah now pictures those survivors themselves going out to the most distant countries to proclaim Yahweh's glory. As in Is 56, Trito-Isaiah again recognises that through acceptance of Yahweh's *torah* and *mishpat* these foreigners become full members of the cult community. Consequently they are even eligible for the priesthood. Nationhood is now of no concern to Yahweh: obedience to *torah* alone determines a man's acceptability. Further, as in Is 51:6, Trito-Isaiah argues that even when the existing creation has passed away, and a new one is made, the promise to Israel, the priest nation to the world, will endure with 'all flesh' coming to worship in Jerusalem (comp. Zech 14:16ff).

The vision of the foreign nations coming to Jerusalem to learn Yahweh's *torah* and the resultant paradisal peace is again pictured in Is 2:2-4 also found in Mic 4:1-4 with an additional verse. The history of the composition of this oracle remains a matter of dispute. Its striking inconsistency with the rest of Micah usually leads commentators to deny its authenticity to that prophet: but there are still many who would regard it as genuinely Isaianic as the additional note Is 2:1 asserts. But its close relationship to the new universalistic thought of Deutero- and Trito-Isaiah makes such an identification highly implausible.[26]

The oracle is modelled on a picture of the nations streaming to Jerusalem to celebrate the annual pilgrimage feast of Tabernacles at the centre of which lay the proclamation of Yahweh's *torah*. But a number of commentators here interpret *torah* not in the Deuteronomic sense, followed in Deutero-Isaiah, of a comprehensive term expressing the complete will of Yahweh, but rather its earlier though continued use (Hag 2:11-13) as a specific instruction for a particular case.[27] The foreign nations are then seen as individual plaintiffs coming to Zion to have their individual cases heard by Yahweh, and after his judgment, return home. But in my view this is too narrow an interpretation for in Is 2:3 (Mic 4:2) the nations specifically indicate that they seek general instruction in Yahweh's ways—that is how in any given situation which may confront them they are to act. Only with such knowledge can they be said to walk in his paths. Is 2:4 (Mic 4:3) is not to be interpreted as in a temporal sequence with the preceding verse, but rather as a statement of consequence. In Is 2:3 (Mic 4:2) the nations come to Zion for general instruction in Yahweh's *torah*, just as long before Israel had gone to the mountain of the Lord, Sinai, for a similar comprehensive body of teaching (Ex 19ff). Is 2:4 (Mic 4:3) then points out that the nations' acceptance of the validity of Yahweh's law immediately results in an enormous increase in the area of his jurisdiction. Further, since the nations now become part of the one people of God subject to his *torah*, war now becomes irrelevant. Law thus achieves its avowed aim of ensuring absolute *shalom*, that is order, harmony and peace over all mankind. Instead of agricultural implements being forged into weapons of war, each man can now cultivate his own land in the knowledge that eternal peace reigns, a prophecy reversed in Joel 3:10. Yahweh himself and not a Davidic king performs the role of the ideal Messianic prince (Is 11) ensuring world peace and justice, and so, as the additional verse in Mic 4:4 points out, freeing the farmers from fear of military call-up (1 Kings 4:25). Jerusalem thus becomes the centre of a transformed world no longer concerned for power and domination, but only that Yahweh's will might prevail. Here we see her in effect fulfilling her role as priest to the world.

But the promise of this oracle depends solely on the grace of Yahweh. It is not man's to achieve but results from the prior action of Yahweh in establishing the primacy of Mount Zion. The oracle is strictly eschatological: it will be realised in the latter days, not just in the distant future (Gen 49:1; Num 24:14), but in Yahweh's one last act of grace whereby his kingdom will be inaugurated and history brought to its goal. The coming of the kingdom depends then entirely on divine initiative. Israel of herself cannot inaugurate it. But the possibility of such an inauguration will depend on their being a faithful mediator, a new Moses, who will be available on the eschatological day to act as Yahweh's servant. Hence the importance of Is 2:5 (Mic 4:5). Israel's part is to provide that continuity of faith without which Yahweh cannot bring about the eschatological reign of peace, but the gift of that reign and the time of its dawning depends entirely on Yahweh, and on Yahweh alone.

It was this concern to ensure the survival of a distinct people of Yahweh which dominated the reforms of Ezra and Nehemiah in connection with mixed marriages (Ezra 9–10; Neh 13). Whether we have a description of two separate historical occasions or whether the same traditions have been related to both Ezra and Nehemiah need not detain us.[28] In order to justify their action, both make direct appeal to Deuteronomic law (Dt 7:1-6; 23:3-5). Indeed the Chronicler specifically adopts the Deuteronomic idea that the return from exile marked a second entry into the promised land. Those returning were to separate themselves entirely from the peoples of the lands—interpreted as if they included all foreigners (Ezra 9:1). It is those who have been through the exilic experience who constitute the true Israel and in whom hope for the future lies. So it is the returning exiles who dedicate the rebuilt temple though they are joined by those who forsake the pollutions of the people of the land (Ezra 6:21). Seeing the threat to the survival of Israel as a distinct people, accentuated by the fact that she was no longer a political entity but only a worshipping community, and illustrated for example in the loss of knowledge of that community's language (Neh 13:23-24), Ezra and Nehemiah took drastic action against all foreign elements. Marriages were in future to be an internal Jewish matter, (comp. Mal 2:10-12) foreign wives were to be divorced (Ezra 9–10; Neh 12:23-29), and those of mixed blood removed from the community (Ezra 10:44; Neh 13:1-3). *Torah*, most probably now to be understood as the Pentateuch, and again interpreted as the full expression of Yahweh's will, was alone to define membership of Israel.

Yet it must not be thought that these reforms entirely put the clock back by a return to the Deuteronomic ghetto theology. For particularism and universalism are not terms which cannot co-exist. On the contrary, the basic post-exilic ideal was of a particular nation, Israel, acting as priest to all other nations. It was through Israel faithfully maintaining her identity in obedience to *torah* that Yahweh in his own time would be able to bring all men into that communion which he willed for them. While the universalistic eschatological hope of Israel found in Deutero-Isaiah, Trito-Isaiah and Proto-Zechariah was of no immediate concern to Ezra and Nehemiah, their action did nothing to invalidate it. Indeed their particularist stance based on strict adherence to *torah* enable Israel to survive the Seleucid period and kept that eschatological hope alive.

Nor despite Nehemiah's appeal to Dt 23:3-5 (Neh 13:1) must it be thought that individual proselytes could not be incorporated into Israel as envisaged by Trito-Isaiah (Is 56). While marriages were to be made within the worshipping community of Israel, those who were prepared to separate themselves from the pollution of the peoples of the land by accepting Yahweh's *torah* would find themselves members of that community (Ezra 6:21). While one cannot imagine that in the time of Ezra and Nehemiah there would have been many converts to Judaism, by continuing to insist on obedience to *torah* as the sole criterion for membership of the chosen people, the reformers paradoxically left the way open for foreign converts from future generations.

It has, however, often been alleged that in the books of Ruth and Jonah we have a direct challenge to the particularist theology of Ezra and Nehemiah. The former tells the story of a Moabite woman who adopts Judaism and becomes the great grandmother of the greatest hero in Israel's history, king David. The latter depicts the repentence of the most wicked city in the world, Nineveh, in response to the preaching of

Yahweh's prophet. Those who regard these books as missionary tracts then argue that their authors sought to imply that Israel ought to be making greater efforts to bring knowledge of Yahweh to those outside Judaism, for who could tell what the consequences of such evangelism might be.

Examination of the book of Ruth does not substantiate this view. In the first place the genealogy of 4:18-22 has been incorporated into the book either from 1 Chron 2:4-15 or derived from the same source. Nor is 4:17b a genuine part of the narrative. For at this point the story requires that the name of the child should be specifically related to Naomi. It is therefore clear that the original tale had no connection at all with David.[29]

Second, the total lack of any reflection on the significance of marriage with a foreigner—for or against—(comp. 1:4; 4:6) rules out the conclusion that the book was a polemical attack on the mixed marriage policy of Ezra and Nehemiah. At the time the book was written, such marriages were entirely acceptable and unremarkable. Indeed the point of the tale lies not in Ruth's foreignness, but her faithfulness which the former only serves to heighten. The story comes from the same sort of popular wisdom background as the legend of Job which forms the framework to the Biblical book. Adversity faithfully endured will be richly rewarded.

In my view, the book of Ruth is clearly post-exilic. But since the narrative shows no bias over mixed marriages one way or the other, it could hardly have been compiled in the period following the reforms of Ezra and Nehemiah. Further the fact that the heroine is of all races a Moabitess (comp. Neh 13:1) suggests to me that it most probably comes from the time following the deliberate rejection of Dt 23:2-9 by Trito-Isaiah (Is 56). It would therefore reflect the period before the reforms of Ezra and Nehemiah when foreign marriages were widely entered into (Mal 2:10-12) and, despite the Deuteronomic law, a foreigner was encouraged to take his place in the Jewish worshipping community (Is 56).

The result of Jonah's announcement of Nineveh's imminent punishment is the repentence of its king and people, and their pardon by Yahweh. But nowhere is it said that they were called to repent of their idolatry nor that they embraced Yahwism. Nor is the sacrifice of the sailors and their vows to be interpreted as a sign of conversion. In the heat of the moment they try to propitiate a dangerous god. But there is no indication that they rejected their former gods for the sole worship of Yahweh. They merely acted prudently. And, despite the clearly didactic nature of the book, it contains no evidence at all that it was written in opposition to the measures taken by Ezra and Nehemiah.[30] Indeed the situation envisaged by the book seems akin to that in Jer 18:7-8 where Yahweh declares his intention to pardon a nation if that nation turns from its evil. Without saying anything about monotheism, Jeremiah's concern is to emphasise the world-wide authority of Yahweh. He is a free agent and can condemn and pardon whom he wills. The same idea of overall authority is present in Amos 9:7f. In my view, in the book of Jonah we are very much closer to this earlier thought about Yahweh's authority over the nations—seen again, of course, in his use of Cyrus—than to the universalistic passages of Deutero-Isaiah, Trito-Isaiah and Proto-Zechariah which all interpret Yahweh's relationship to the foreign nations in terms of Israel herself acting as the go-between. It is thus Yahweh's sovereignty rather than his magnanimity which is the prime stress of Jonah which the incident of the gourd further emphasises. What occasioned the need to assert this?

Now the ironical aspect of the book of Jonah is that the Assyrian capital was, of course, destroyed by the Babylonians in accordance with Yahweh's plans (Is 10:12-15, 24-27; 14:24-27). But the author of Jonah is clearly countering the claim that another Nineveh threatened by Yahweh with destruction has not been destroyed but surprisingly pardoned. In other words the book indicates Israel's sense of insecurity and doubt in the power of her God when faced with the continued presence of a certain heathen nation which confronts her. The author of Jonah meets this despair with the assertion that the world situation, however unexpected, is all part of Yahweh's plan: he has everything in his control.[31] Can we be more specific still? I believe we can.

Deutero-Isaiah's prophecy had asserted that Yahweh was master of world events. Even now Israel's deliverance was being put into effect and Babylon would be destroyed (Is 47:1ff. Comp. Is 41:11ff; 51:23). But in fact this destruction had not occurred. Instead the Persian prince, Cyrus, had been welcomed as a liberator by those conservative Babylonians who had disapproved of the policies of Nabonidus. There can be little doubt that the insignificant nature of the return from exile, the failure to rebuild the temple, and the 'escape' of Babylon from punishment led to considerable uncertainty among loyal Yahwists. In my view the aim of the author of Jonah was to counter such uncertainty. Thus he asserts that the God of grace who had not forgotten Israel in Babylon, but who had delivered him from exile, was still in control of world events. Babylon had not escaped Yahweh's punishment through her own strength or the strength of her gods: Yahweh had pardoned her. It might be argued that there is no evidence of any Babylonian repentence. But the fact that the older influential groups ousted by

Nabonidus, including the priests of Marduk, welcomed Cyrus, Yahweh's anointed, would amply justify a picture of repentence and account for Yahweh's pardon of the city which Cyrus could then enter in peace. After all Deutero-Isaiah makes very strong claims for Cyrus though he never became a Yahwist. The purpose of the author of Jonah is then clear. Like the author of Ruth he seeks to encourage faithfulness in Yahweh whose providence can be trusted and whose grace knows no bounds. Further, again like Ruth, the book may also derive from scribal wisdom circles. If my reasoning is correct it ought then to be attributed to the period following Deutero-Isaiah whose theology of the sovereignty of Yahweh over history it upholds. In this period the lot of Israel remained desperate and hostility to Babylon, by no means as violent in Deutero-Isaiah as elsewhere (Jer 50–51; Is 13–14; 21) continued (comp. Zechariah). Thus the didactic nature of Jonah can be explained without any recourse to a Jewish opposition party to the reforms of Ezra and Nehemiah of which there is no Biblical evidence.

Finally, we should note that this interpretation finds support from the one Old Testament reference to the prophet Jonah outside the book called after him. For in 2 Kings 14:25 it is recorded that Jeroboam II restored the borders of Israel in accordance with the prophecy of Jonah the son of Amittai. In other words this unique Biblical reference to Jonah's ministry concerns the proclamation of Yahweh's sovereignty over the nations and his control of the extent of their territories. And just as the historic Jonah had sought to reassure his insecure contemporaries about their future (2 Kings 14:26), so the book of Jonah does the same for their successors. Yahweh is lord of history and despite any appearances to the contrary remains totally master of events. The book of Jonah is then quite properly included among the prophets even though it contains no specific oracles.

In conclusion then my investigation confirms de Boer, Snaith and Martin-Achard's assertion that Israel was neither summoned to nor contemplated an active missionary role to the foreign nations, and Ruth and Jonah are not to be understood as protests against this lack of evangelisation. But this does not mean that post-exilic prophecy is to be interpreted as narrowly nationalistic concerned only with Israel's vindication and exaltation over the nations. On the contrary, this prophecy repeatedly looks forward to Yahweh's redemption of the whole world. But in order that Yahweh can realise this universalistic hope—and it is clearly recognised that it is entirely his affair—sufficient of his people must remain faithful to him to enable Israel to fulfil her role as priest nation to the world. Thus the concern of all post-exilic theology is to ensure the survival of that faithful community in the face of so much discouragement and unfulfilled hopes. The only way of achieving this was through demanding strict adherence to Yahweh's *torah* and *mishpat*. And in acceptance of its authority by the faithful remnant ultimately lay the key to the unity of all mankind and the realisation of the goal of Israelite history in the return to the paradisal state of Eden which as a result of post-exilic prophecy would embrace all men (Is 11: 10). Yahweh's *torah* and *mishpat* are not then as in pre-exilic times concerned only with maintaining Israel's election: rather they are of universal significance, and are aptly termed 'a light to the peoples'.

NOTES

1. Comp. A. Phillips, *Ancient Israel's Criminal Law: A New Approach to the Decalogue*, Oxford 1970; E. W. Nicholson, *Exodus and Sinai in History and Tradition*, Oxford 1973.
2. B. Lindars, 'Torah in Deuteronomy', in *Words and Meanings* (Eds. P. R. Ackroyd and Lindars), Cambridge 1968, pp. 117-136.
3. M. Weinfeld, *Deuteronomy and the Deuteronomic School*, Oxford 1972; H. W. Gilmer, *The If-You Form in Israelite Law*, Missoula, Montana 1975.
4. J. B. Pritchard (Ed.), *Ancient Near Eastern Texts*, Princeton 1955[2], p. 161a.
5. Ibid., p. 178b.
6. Phillips, *Deuteronomy, Cambridge Bible Commentary*, Cambridge 1973, p. 32.
7. Comp. W. Zimmerli, *The Law and the Prophets*, Oxford 1965. pp. 86ff; Phillips, *God B.C.*, Oxford 1977, pp. 43ff.
8. P. A. H. de Boer, 'Second Isaiah's Message', in *OTS* 9 (1956) 80-101.
9. N. H. Snaith, 'The Servant of the Lord in Deutero-Isaiah', in *Studies in Old Testament Prophecy* (Ed. H. H. Rowley), Edinburgh 1950, pp. 187-200; and 'Isaiah 40–66: A Study of the Teaching of Second Isaiah and Its Consequences', in *Studies on the Second Part of the Book of Isaiah, VTS* 14 (1967) 154-165.
10. R. Martin-Achard, *A Light to the Nations*, Edinburgh and London 1962.
11. Op. cit., p. 90.
12. Op. cit., p. 13.
13. J. Lindblom, *Prophecy in Ancient Israel*, Oxford 1963, pp. 427f.
14. For the history of the study of the servant songs, comp. C. R. North, *The Suffering Servant in Deutero-Isaiah*, Oxford 1956[2]; Rowley, 'The Servant of the Lord in the Light of Three Decades of Criticism', in *The Servant of the Lord and Other Essays on the Old Testament*, London 1952; Zimmerli and J. Jeremias, *The Servant of God*, Studies in Biblical Theology 20, London 1957.
15. A Bentzen, *King and Messiah*, London 1953; G. von Rad, *Old Testament Theology*, II, London and Edinburgh 1965, pp. 250ff.

16. Phillips, *Ancient Israel's Criminal Law*, pp. 167ff., *Deuteronomy*, p. 6.
17. Ibid., p. 30. Comp. Mt 4:8f; Lk 14:18. This method of conveying land is also found in Roman law.
18. In Ps 106:32-33 an attempt is made to reconcile the two traditions.
19. Many commentators have sought to excise 'Israel' from Is 49:3 as a late interpolation (e.g. S. Mowinckel, *He That Cometh*, Oxford 1956, pp. 462ff.; C. Westermann, *Isaiah 40–66*, London 1969, pp. 208ff.). But manuscript evidence would argue for its retention (comp. North, *The Second Isaiah*, Oxford 1964, p. 187f.).
20 I. Lewy, 'Dating of Covenant Code Sections on Humaneness and Righteousness', in *VT* 7 (1957) 322ff. These provisions could have been the work of wisdom circles and may well be associated with the period of the establishment of the Davidic monarchy. Compare my *Ancient Israel's Criminal Law*, pp. 158ff., and my review of Gilmer, *JTS* 27 (1976) 425.
21. H. Torczyner, 'Presidential Address', in *JPOS* 16 (1936) 7.
22. J. Skinner, *Isaiah ii, Cambridge Bible* (revised), Cambridge 1917, p. 32,
23. Op. cit., p. 14.
24. Ibid., p. 15.
25. L. Kohler, *Hebrew Man*, London 1956, p. 37ff.
26. Compare O. Kaiser, *Isaiah 1-12*, London 1972, p. 24f; J. L. Mays, *Micah*, London 1976, pp. 95f. and the literature cited by both authors.
27. E. g. Lindars, op. cit., p. 121; Mays, op. cit., p. 97.
28. Compare R. J. Coggins, *The Books of Ezra and Nehemiah, Cambridge Bible Commentary*, Cambridge 1976.
29. Kaiser, *Introduction to the Old Testament*, Oxford 1975, p. 191f.
30. Two recent studies of Jonah have both rejected this interpretation: R. E. Clements, 'The Purpose of the Book of Jonah', in *VTS* 28 (1975) 16-28; G. I. Emmerson, 'Another Look at the Book of Jonah', in *ET* 88 (1976) 86-88. See further, S. D. F. Goiten, 'Some Observations on Jonah', in *JPOS* 17 (1937) 63-77.
31. At a different level this is also the point of the beginning of the story in which Jonah seeks to avoid an unpleasant and dangerous task. Ackroyd, *Exile and Restoration*, London 1968, p. 244f. has revived the suggestion that the incident of the great fish should be interpreted allegorically. Jonah represents Israel swallowed up by the fish, Babylon.

THEOLOGY OF REDEMPTION IN THE FATHERS

Gabriel Daly, O.S.A.

In his book, *The Christian Ministry in Africa*, Bishop Bengt Sundkler gives an account of an Easter sermon by a celebrated Zulu preacher. The preacher had described the first Adam bearing a heavy load of suffering brought upon him by his sin. This description led into the high point of the sermon:

> Zulus, men and women, consider that incredible joy, that indescribable jubilation which filled Adam's heart on the First Easter Morning, as the Hero of Heaven came in through the Gate of Heaven, with His Crown of Thorns, now a brilliant Crown of Victory, walking the central aisle in the heavenly Temple, straight up to the throne of the Almighty. There He gave His report that from this day Satan and Sin and Death had been overcome. For now He, the Second Adam, had won the victory.
>
> And the First Adam had peace.[1]

This, Sundkler comments, is living African theology. F. W. Dillistone, who cites Sundkler's book, goes on to remark that this sermon is rooted in the archetypal myths of African culture and resonates movingly with tribal life. He concludes: 'The parallels between the Church in Africa today and the Church in Syria and Asia Minor in the first three centuries are not hard to discern.'[2] Indeed the parallels of which Dr Dillistone speaks can be found not merely in the first three centuries. That Zulu sermon could have been effectively preached anywhere in Western Europe during the first Christian millenium.

I have asked myself why I could not have preached it to a suburban congregation on Easter morning. It is biblically based and fully in keeping with patristic teaching. Perhaps it is lack of faith on my part, but I have found no convincing model for speaking about Christ's victory to tribes of urbanised worshippers battling with the anxieties arising out of a culture based on a rapidly developing technology geared to a consumer society.

133

I make this point at the outset of these two lectures because, as Heinrich Ott has remarked, preaching is the conscience of the dogmatic theologian, and no doctrine puts this conscience to the test more than the central Christian doctrine of redemption. Ott, it should be added, also remarks that theology is the conscience of the preacher, which means that if the preacher is to avoid making the sanctified noise that his congregations are conditioned to expect him to make, he must share in the challenges and problems, the excitements and the agonies, of contemporary theology.

I have just spoken of 'the Christian doctrine of redemption'. The word 'redemption' is a metaphor which conveys a meaning only if one is aware of, and sensitive to, a certain type of language. Two conditions are necessary for this type of language to speak effectively. First, one must accept that non-literal language can convey truth as authentically as literal language—indeed, in some cases more authentically. Second one must have some kind of experience, either direct or imaginative, of the field from which the metaphor is drawn. Unless there is some experience of captivity, it is hard to see how the metaphor of being bought back can have much relevance or impact.

To avoid begging any linguistic questions, therefore, I should have said 'the Christian doctrine of the work and achievement of Christ'. Even in this amended and prosaic form, the phrase is problematical in that it uses the word 'doctrine' and not 'proclamation'. We need to advert to the fact that there is no speculatively developed Church doctrine of the work of Christ as there is of his person. Soteriology is one of the few instances of a central theological subject in which one cannot make the customary contrast between biblical simplicity and existential directness on the one hand and the abstractions and lucubrations of hellenised dogma on the other.

I hope I am not too wide of the mark in noting that the main New Testament teaching on the work of Christ is to be found in (1) the kerygmatic passages of Paul with Luke's account of the first apostolic sermons in Acts, (2) developed Pauline teaching on the death and resurrection of Jesus, (3) Gospel pericopes attributed to Jesus himself by the evangelists, and (4) the Letter to the Hebrews with its cultic assimilation of Jesus' death to Temple worship. The kerygma tells us that Christ died for our sins; that this death took place in accordance with scriptural expectation; that Jesus was delivered up 'according to the definite plan and foreknowledge of God' (Acts 2:23). Paul's developed theological teaching on the meaning of Christ's death is conveyed in a series of metaphors borrowed from various fields of human experience. The basic terms are reconciliation, redemption or liberation; expiation or propitiation (*hilasterion* has proved to be one of the more dangerous terms in the hands of moralistic and legalistic teachers); and justification. The Letter to the Hebrews adds the cultic notions of 'offering', 'sacrifice', and the deeply emotive noun 'blood'. Finally, as an instance of a saying attributed to Jesus which was to have an extensive influence on patristic thinking, we have the Markan pericope 'For the Son of Man also came not to be served but to serve, and to give his life as a ransom for many' (Mk 10:45).

That there is no philosophically developed dogma of redemption is a matter of continuing interest for systematic theology. The Greek mind which addressed itself eagerly to the ontological subtleties of the problem of the person of Christ could find nothing comparable in the meaning of Christ's salvific acts. In this curious phenomenon we have a reminder that the deepest spiritual truths do not necessarily lend themselves to purely rational discourse. The doctrine of redemption has been remarkably resistant to development by speculative accumulation and the normal ebb and flow of theological dialectic. Unlike the doctrine of the person of Christ the doctrine of the meaning of his passion and death seems to have its receptive centre in us at a pre-conceptual level. Myth rather than metaphysics is its most appropriate vehicle of expression. There seems to be something inescapably primitive, archetypal, and primordial about its message to us. Bishop John Taylor in his fine book, *The Go-Between God*, makes a point about the Holy Spirit which can fittingly be applied to the salvific work of Jesus.

> The Greek philosophers supposed that pure reason was the only element in man that could aspire to know absolute reality, which was why they found it virtually impossible to believe in a total incarnation of God. But the mystery religions kept alive an older, truer and more dangerous knowledge of the meeting of God with man. There is more of Dionysius than Apollo in the Holy Spirit.[3]

Perhaps the New Testament writers, especially Paul and the author of Hebrews, may be said to have shown their instinctive appreciation of this by the sort of language they chose to convey the transcendent meaning of the terrible death which Jesus underwent. We should be especially careful how we distinguish between fact and interpretation in the theology. We cannot, simply by stripping away the interpretative element of the various methods of presentation, arrive at a simple literal biblical truth. There is, furthermore, no Christian teaching so difficult to demythologise as that of redemption. Get rid of the myths, and you find that the core of the teaching has gone too. In point of fact each of the Pauline models is a myth *in nuce*. Fact and interpretation are inseparable here. The doctrine of redemption makes its appeal directly to the untutored mind, while it may leave the sophisticate at something of a loss.

The hellenistic mind was more at home with the notion of a God who *is* than with that of a God who *acts* in history. From their hellenistic background the Eastern Fathers derived something like an obsession with divine immutability and impassibility. The doctrine of redemption, however, clearly postulates divine interventive action in and through Christ. The dilemma is to some extent met by the Antiochene Fathers in their emphasis on the Son of God 'suffering in his human nature'. The danger here, as with all Antiochene theology, was a dualistic Christ whose godhead is in some sense a spectator of his manhood's suffering. Essentialist metaphysics found its truest and most characteristic expression in the Alexandrian preoccupation with the unity of Christ. A theology with monophysite tendencies and a strongly substantialist ontology will tend to view *ensarkosis* as itself redemptive. The historical acts of the enfleshed Son of God are simply overshadowed by the blinding ontological glory of the hypostatic union.

Greek thinking from Irenaeus onwards is preoccupied with *corporate* considerations. Redemption comes to human *nature*. What Christ achieves *in* his human nature becomes an achievement *of* that nature. As Irenaeus puts it, 'In the second Adam we were reconciled, becoming obedient to God'.[4] This would appear to be a logical extrapolation from Pauline 'Christ-mysticism', though one might also argue that something of Paul's personalism is lost in the translation into hellenistic thought. In this respect, however, Irenaeus is not the most typical of the Greek Fathers, since he has a stronger concept of history than had most of his patristic successors.

St Irenaeus of Lyons was something of an intellectual maverick who still resists the customary labels. A Greek translated to the West, and arguably the first Father to merit the description 'theologian' as distinct from philosopher-turned-Christian, Irenaeus has disconcerted both Liberal Protestants and scholastic Roman Catholics. Any religious thinker who can do that is worthy of attention. Dean Hastings Rashdall regarded Irenaeus as 'a thinker of no very high order—not very acute and not very consistent'.[5] who was concerned with 'the production of striking and edifying parallelism or symbolisms'.[6] Jean Riviere, an historical theologian sensitive to the icy winds of anti-modernist Catholicism, described Irenaeus as a man of 'somewhat unstable thought'.[7] Gustaf Aulèn calls him 'the Schleiermacher of the second century'.[8] Berthold Altaner thinks that he was 'in a certain sense the Father of Catholic dogmatics'.[9] Most commentators would agree with F. L. Cross that he was 'the most considerable Christian theologian of the second century'.[10] Irenaeus's thought is most satisfyingly unfinished and lacking in strict logical consistency—a fact which not infrequently contributes to the enduring readability of certain theologians. (The history of theology is replete with theologians who were impeccably logical and insufferably dull.) Irenaeus was a biblically-minded theologian with an undoctrinaire coating of hellenistic culture. To quote Rashdall again, Irenaeus 'seems always engaged in tentative efforts at exploration which fail to satisfy even his own mind'.[11] Such modesty has not always seemed as becoming in a theologian as contemporary theological tribulations have made fashionable.

Irenaeus made two notable contributions to patristic theology in general and to soteriology in particular. The first was his preoccupation with a divine plan. More historically sensitive than later Greek Fathers, he developed at length the New Testament kerygmatic insight into the need to recognise that the life, death, and resurrection of Jesus must be seen against the background of a divine dispensation which governs all history from the creation to the parousia. Like Hippolytus and Tertullian, Irenaeus distinguished between *theologia* and *oikonomia*. Irenaeus's God is delightfully free of the arbitrary severity which we find in many of the later Fathers and medieval theologians. God does not need man, says Irenaeus. This divine independence, however, issues not in holy despotism, but in loving generosity. Everything God does for man, from creation onwards, is done 'not because he had need of man, but that he might have a being on whom to lavish his benefits'.[12]

The calm serenity of Irenaeus's soteriology is the counterpart of his understanding of what came to be known as original sin and is a reminder to us of the mutual interpenetration of one's theology of sin and one's theology of atonement. A purely ethical view of sin will often have as its counterpart a penal or forensic view of redemption. A God who is angered by sin will usually turn out to be a God who needs to be appeased by blood sacrifice. Irenaeus is splendidly free of this projection onto God of man's meanest and most spiteful tendencies. Adam and Eve were seduced by the Serpent. This was no difficult task for the Serpent, for they were children.[13] The First Sin was one of immaturity. Adam and Eve were induced to jump the gun and forestall God's plan for them and their descendants. God's reaction to the First Sin is not anger at man's rebellion but compassion for his weakness. And so God ' l a plan of salvation like an architect'.[14] Gently removing man from Paradise and the Tree of Life, so that man would not be eternally imprisoned in the consequences of his transgression, God intromitted death as a merciful release.[15] Man would now have to undergo a programme of recuperative education under which he would learn 'the knowledge of moral discipline, then attaining to the resurrection from the dead, and learning by experience what is the source of his deliverance', would 'always live in a state of gratitude to the Lord'.[16]

Christ is the centrepiece of this divine programme. Man had been created in the image and likeness of God. It was God's plan now to show in Christ what it *means* in a visible manner to be created in the image of God. Here we meet Irenaeus's second great contribution to soteriology, namely, his concept of *anakephalaiosis*. There has been some debate over the correspondence, or lack of it, between the teaching of Ephesians 1:10 and Irenaeus's most characteristic insight. Since the Pauline concept of recapitulation is itself a largely undeveloped one, the point is hardly crucial.

By becoming a man the Word of God, says Irenaeus, 'recapitulated in himself all the dispersed peoples dating back to Adam. . .'[17] and procured for us a comprehensive salvation. As mediator between God and man Christ was able 'by his connection with both parties to bring them again into peace and friendship, presenting man to God and revealing God to man'.[18] By passing through every age of human growth from childhood, through youth, to full manhood Christ redeemed humanity in all its stages.[19] Humanity—to us perhaps inevitably an abstraction—was to Irenaeus a term denoting the social solidarity of all men and women of every age. A great deal of Liberal Protestant discomfort with Irenaeus's soteriolgoy centred on its alleged suggestion of automatic redemption with no strong ethical ingredient: human nature is redeemed by its sheer conjunction with divine nature. Harnack actually accused Irenaeus of 'physicalism'. The fact is we have here a soteriological principle which was to dominate Greek, especially Alexandrian, theology: only what is assumed can be redeemed. The point was later to be made against the Alexandrians themselves when they seemed to be suggesting that in Christ the divine nature took the place of the human soul. If the human soul was not assumed, the Antiochene theologians claimed, it was not redeemed.

Irenaeus's doctrine of recapitulation set a pattern which Alexandrian soteriology consistently followed: The Incarnation is itself redemptive. The West has never seemed at ease with the doctrine of *theiosis* or divinisation. Abstract, mystical and ontological, with an apparent smack of pantheism about it, the doctrine of deification does not really speak convincingly to literal and legalistic minds such as are not uncommonly to be found in the West. Western Catholicism has traditionally given it lip-service before switching the drama to the courtroom, where the real business is done. Protestantism has traditionally disliked its mysticism and its alleged lack of ethical seriousness. Many commentators have felt that in some way it weakens the role of the Cross and consequently the glory of the resurrection. Perhaps the best answer to this charge is to note that in teachers like Irenaeus the Incarnation, Passion, and Resurrection of Christ are all of a piece, all taken up into the one sweep of divine love for man.

Irenaeus's theological scheme is replete with parallelisms and symbolic correspondences. He delights in the Adam/Christ parallelism, a device which Rashdall disliked but which is nonetheless of considerable importance for keeping the theology of salvation in close relationship with the theology of sin. Sin, as Irenaeus sees it, is a malady from which man needs to be healed rather than a crime for which he merits punishment and purification. Before turning to the characteristically western concern with divine penology, I want to reflect a moment on an area of patristic soteriology which has embarrassed, exasperated, or amused commentators for a long time. I refer to the 'Devil's rights', or 'transactional', theory of atonement.

The metaphor of ransom figures prominently in the New Testament. 'The Son of Man came not to be served but to serve and to give his life as a ransom for many.' *Lutron* and *apolutrosis* are basic terms in New Testament soteriology. They also serve as a grim warning of what can happen if figurative language is driven too hard or allowed to collapse into literalism. The biblical writers were content to deploy the metaphor of ransom without specifying the recipient. Not so the Fathers. They fell upon the question with relish. Origen claimed that since the ransom could not be paid to God, the only other candidate was the Devil.[20] Gregory of Nyssa prefers the notions of the Devil's deception. One tends to be amused today by Nyssa's view of the humanity of Christ as bait and the divinity as fish-hook.[21] Nineteenth century liberal commentators were profoundly shocked by this attribution to God of immoral, or at least frivolous, behaviour. There is a good deal of evidence to suggest that the Fathers had a sense of humour totally lacking in the liberals. The Fathers genuinely enjoyed the spectacle of the deceiver deceived. There is a certain low humour running through the patristic theme of the Devil's deception which continued to engage the medieval mind and fascinate its imagination. The role of the devil was one feature of Greek soteriology which passed over to the West and enjoyed a thousand-year run, until Anselm put paid to it at the turn of the eleventh century and gave us in its stead the grim theory of satisfaction. I shall return to this shortly.

In the meantime let us look at what happened when the West turned its mind to the theology of redemption. Protestant and Anglican historical theology has tended to emphasise the contrast between Eastern and Western soteriology. Catholicism, notoriously weak in historical perspective, saw no point, and much danger, in contrasting the attitudes and preoccupations of different schools of theology. What mattered was, after all, the seamless robe of Tradition. Truth cannot be at odds with itself, especially divinely guaranteed truth. With the break-up of mandatory scholasticism at and during the Second Vatican Council, a renaissance of historical theology began to take place within Catholicism. It is therefore rather surprising, to say the least, to find Leopold Sabourin, who partners Stanislas Lyonnet in a biblical-patristic study, *Sin, Redemption, and Sacrifice*, remarking: 'An impartial study of the history of dogma reveals that substantial agreement characterises the development of the doctrine of redemption in the two great Christian traditions, the Greek and the Latin.'[22] Leaving to one side the tendentious epithet 'impartial', we are faced with the still more tendentious phrase 'substantial agreement'. Not even Harnack had suggested *substantial* disagreement between the Greek and Latin doctrines of redemption. Nevertheless that hypothetical and Utopian creature, the impartial student, is forced by the evidence to concede, as Sabourin does not concede, that the points of emphasis and the theological preoccupations and language do indeed diverge as between East and West. The Eastern theology of sin borrows its characteristic models from pathology; while the Western theology of sin borrows its characteristic models from the world of crime. Accordingly, Eastern soteriology conducts the patient to the hospital; while Western soteriology lands the criminal in the dock of a courtroom. The gentle and attractive heresy of *apocatastasis* is characteristically Eastern. The harsh and repellant orthodoxy of double predestination is characteristically Western. Gregory of Nyssa's fishhook may be crude imagery, but Gregory's fisherman saves the whole catch. Augustine's mousetrap is no less crude, and, in addition, Augustine allows us to understand that much of the food saved from the mouse is destined to putrify anyway.

It has often been pointed out that many of the West's leading theologians were trained as lawyers. Legal models and metaphors have, of course, their rightful claim in Christian theology. After all, much of Paul's language was forensic. It had to be, since he was combatting pharisaical legalism. The point at issue is not the presence of legal and forensic figures in the language of Christian theology but their degree of prominence in relationship to other figures. Much depends on how you run your courtroom. Tertullian's judge is unlikely to remand the prisoner for a medical report. Tertullian was a rigorist with regard to post-baptismal sin and, like his fellow-African, Cyprian, an exclusivist in his attitude to the Church. 'Every sin,' says Tertullian, 'is discharged either by pardon or penalty, pardon as the result of chastisement, penalty as the result of condemnation.'[23] The sinner must satisfy the Lord.[24] Although Tertullian is often credited with the introduction of the legal terms 'merit' and 'satisfaction' into the language of theology, he limits their use to personal morality and does not base a Christian soteriology on them. The North Africans, however, did bequeath to Western Christianity an image of God as a stern lawgiver and severe judge, and this image was later to call forth a matching soteriology from the pen of Anselm of Canterbury.

One other matter deserves mention before we turn to Anselm. This matter arises out of what Gustaf Aulèn has called the 'Classic' theory of atonement. Aulèn's book, *Christus Victor*, first published in 1931, was quickly recognised as a work of scholarship and originality.[25] Aulèn tackles his subject historically, but he has two axes to grind. First, he sets out to show that Luther's doctrine of the atonement, if properly understood, is a faithful reflection of the 'Classic' patristic teaching. Secondly, he proposes to repair the damage done to soteriology by Liberal Protestants like Ritschl and Harnack. Aulèn's thesis is that the customary classification of atonement theories into 'objective' and 'subjective' is seriously defective. In effect Aulèn subdivides the so-called 'objective' typing into 'Classic' and 'Latin', while he refers to the 'subjective' type as 'humanistic'.

Critical comment on Aulèn's book has generally agreed that he exaggerates his thesis and does not do full justice either to Anselm or to the Liberal Protestant tradition. Nevertheless his distinction between 'Classic' and 'Latin' has remained consistently stimulating. He outlines the 'Classic' theory as follows:

> ... Incarnation and Redemption belong indissolubly together; God in Christ overcomes the hostile powers which hold man in bondage. At the same time these hostile powers are also the executants of God's will. The patristic theology is dualistic, but it is not an absolute Dualism. The deliverance of man from the power of death and the devil is at the same time his deliverance from God's judgement. God is reconciled by His own act in reconciling the world to himself.
>
> Thus the power of evil is broken; that is to say, not that sin and death no longer exist, but that, the devil having been once for all conquered by Christ, His triumph is in principle universal, and His redemptive work can go forward everywhere, through the Spirit who unites men with God and 'deifies' them. ... It can also be said that death is changed from an enemy to a friend.[26]

141

In effect Aulèn demythologises the demonololy and claims to find under the gothic imagery a profound appreciation of the drama of redemption in which God is always the principal actor. Aulèn is a vigorous opponent of the 'Latin' theory, precisely because in this theory *man* plays an active role and seeks thereby to placate a just and offended God by satisfaction, sacrifice, and merit. In this respect Aulen becomes a forceful apologist for some characteristically Protestant contentions and is consequently in some danger of reading back into patristic and medieval times the convictions and polemics of a later age. Nonetheless one can hardly deny that his theory of a dramatic encounter between God and the forces of evil is a fair summary of general patristic soteriology.

One thing is quite certain. This unrefined and mythopoeic view of redemption fitted early medieval culture like a glove. Rarely can a theological construction have been so in harmony with contemporary culture as the 'Classic' theory of redemption was with the culture of the early middle ages. The sophisticated may be tempted to remark that a dark age deserves a crude theology; but in an age like ours when theology and even liturgy find it extremely difficult to forge a convincing link with contemporary secular culture, we can ill-afford to look with condescension at an age that did so with effortless success. In this respect at least we have something to learn from the so-called dark ages.

Medieval soteriology can be appositely described as 'feudal', since it flourished during the rise and spread of the feudal system across Europe. That system saved European society from anarchy. Its values were masculine in the extreme: military prowess was the supreme achievement of secular life. From a theological standpoint it was an impoverish-, ed age, marked by reference to the few authorities available and by an absence of creative thinking. There were no significant heresies. Much of the patristic heritage was lost. Devotional life, naive and crude, had a rough splendour about it which has a strong appeal for our more sophisticated and more febrile age. The poetry of early medieval Europe is the poetry of the battlefield, of honour satisfied in deeds of arms, of comradeship in war, in the bloody winning and losing of great causes. The warrior-hero was the archetype of noble achievement. His prowess was celebrated in song and story and recited unremittingly in the banquet-halls of the great.

In such an age it was inevitable that soteriology should acquire a martial character more or less devoid of theological refinement but rich in epic grandeur. The Devil came into his own as a foe, malicious, crafty and cruel, pitting his skill in combat against God. Since in this martial atmosphere to die bravely and with honour in a noble cause was the

apotheosis of human achievement, Christian teachers found it natural
and convincing to present redemption in the guise of stark and epic
combat. Christ, the Warrior-Hero, went into battle against Satan. It was
an age which calculated life quantitatively in terms of measurable values,
assigning every freeman his *wergild*, his life-price. (For example, in
Anglo-Saxon England a ceorl's life was valued at 200 shillings, a thegn's
at 1200 shillings.) In such an age the military metaphors of ransom,
blood-price, booty and satisfaction all had a vivid relevance. Some of
the cruder patristic myths were given an enthusiastic run. The deception theme was popular. The acquisition of strict rights by the Devil was
unquestioned and indeed was an indispensable basis for a striking, if
primitive, soteriology.

R. W. Southern, in a brilliant chapter of his book *The Making of the
Middle Ages*, describes the age between the sixth and twelfth centuries
as 'epic', contrasting it with later 'romanticism'.[27] Artistic reproductions
of the crucified Christ during this period portray not a suffering man
but the stylised grandeur of a warrior-hero, the *Rex-Sacerdos*, in the act
of inflicting defeat on the ancient enemy. This *Christus Victor* can be
interestingly contrasted with the *Pantocrator* of Byzantine art. Both are
triumphant; but the Western version has the more difficult task of presenting the paradox of victory on a cross.

The literature of the age was equally epic; and the soteriological
reflection of this world-view is magnificently caught in *The Dream of
the Rood*, described by Dame Helen Gardner as 'a great Romanesque
poem, impregnated with sublime and severe Christian conceptions, and
blending with these the ideals of a pagan culture.'[28] The poet has a
dream in which the Cross, personified and endowed with speech, tells
the story of the crucifixion.

> Far off then I saw
> The King of all mankind coming in great haste,
> With courage keen, eager to climb me.
> I did not dare, against my Lord's dictate,
> To bow down or break, though I beheld tremble
> The earth's four corners. I could easily
> Have felled his foes; yet fixed and firm I stood.
> Then the young Hero—it was God Almighty—
> Strong and steadfast, stripped himself for battle;
> He climbed up on the high gallows, constant in his purpose,
> Mounted it in sight of many, mankind to ransom.[29]

Here, as in the figurative art of the period, we notice the epic serenity
of the act of redemption viewed in cosmic perspective. The grandeur,

nobility, and austerity of the epic vision are especially haunting, if impossibly remote from an age afflicted by the tortured introspection of today.

The main lines of feudal soteriology are quickly drawn. By the sin of disobedience, man withdrew from the service of God and offered fealty to the Devil in an act of *diffidatio*. This meant war; but the war had to be fought by the rules. God could not use his divine power against the Devil who had acquired rights in justice over man. Man was powerless to do anything for himself, and therefore his only hope lay in the Devil's breaking of the rules. Precisely in not discerning the divinity of the God-man the Devil overreached himself. He laid claim in justice to the life of Christ who had never been guilty of *diffidatio*. Thus was the Devil's imperium broken. God was now 'free' to reinstate man.

This soteriological thesis held the field until it was insouciantly dismissed by St Anselm in his *Cur Deus Homo*. Anselm's contribution to the theology of redemption has remained the subject of continuous debate. Anselm had a genius for magnificently flawed arguments which continue to fascinate minds which not merely reject them but are fundamentally uninterested in their subject-matter. Anglo-Saxon philosophy, not otherwise notably interested in religion except as a theatre for logical expertise, delights in the refutation of Anselm's ontological argument for the existence of God. Similarly, it is commonplace for theologians, Catholic as well as Protestant, to criticise Anselm's argument for redemption by the God-man as presented in the *Cur Deus Homo*. Whence did his ideas come—from the feudal world in which he lived, or from Latin patrology? Amid the welter of positions and counter-positions, certain clear and agreed lines can be discerned. To begin with, Anselm demolished at a stroke the theory of redemption which rested on the Devil's rights. Acts of theological demolition can create serious hazards for faith, as we today know only too well. To remove the Devil from his central role in the drama of salvation was to break with tradition and popular religion and consequently to induce a theological and spiritual vacuum. 'The empire of the Devil in nature and supernature was a matter of daily experience: the Devil's empire and the daily breaches made in it by Christ provided the framework of history. The contemplation of God's triumphat strategy satisfied imagination and piety alike.'[30]

In place of the theory of cosmic warfare between God and the Devil Anselm put the theory of satisfaction which, following the best lights of the age, aimed at being strictly rational. The cultural background remained feudal but became much less epic. The courtroom replaced the battlefield. Anselm's soteriological thinking is dominated by reflection upon the damage done to God's majesty and honour by sin. He is extremely severe on any attempt to take lightly the divine justice or the offence given to it by sin. Every effort to take a more benign view is met by the stern words *'nondum considerasti quanti ponderis sit peccatum'*.[31]

The main lines of the Anselmian argument are well known: Man was created for the blessedness which comes of total submission to the will of God. But man disobeyed, thus offending against the justice and honour of God. The situation could be remedied only by a satisfaction greater than the disobedience. But man has nothing supererogatory to offer God, since anything he is able to offer he already *owes* to God. Only God can make the sort of reparation (*satisfactio*) called for. But there is no obligation (*debitum*) on God to do so. Hence we reach an impasse: Man *ought* to make retribution but cannot. God alone *can* make the necessary reparation but has no obligation to do so. The stalemate is broken by the offering of the God-man; and the question posed in Anselm's title is answered.

Anselm's soteriology was thus a striking essay in theological relevance to his own age. It is perhaps too easy to react in disfavour today against precisely those elements in the feudal theory which were most relevant to their time. They spoke to their age about realities which transcend the ability of any age to give them permanent expression. There is permanent significance in Anselm's attempt to show 'that there is nothing arbitrary in God'.[32] The problem is that words like 'justice', 'honour', and 'satisfaction' can be made to sound grimly calculating when they are detached from the culture which provided them. Especially do they lose their austere grandeur when they are thought of not as martial and governmental, but as commercial, models. It is arguably no accident that the rise of banking and other sophisticated forms of commerce in the later middle ages coincided with a decline in theology. Feudal contractual customs offer some possibilities as theological models. The contractual arrangements of commerce sound a note of dissonance with the gospel from the start. If salvation is seen as the final outcome of paying off a mortgage throughout life, it becomes virtually impossible to forge a theology of faith and grace as pure gift.

As a link between this and my next paper, and as an illustration of how a traditional soteriological concept can be reinterpreted, I want to draw attention to a couple of fascinating, though undeveloped, pages from Paul Tillich's *Systematic Theology* which treat the topic of divine justice in a manner which maintains a link with Christian tradition while avoiding the cold moralism of a literal interpretation.[33] We need the concept of divine justice, Tillich remarks, in order to avoid a sort of random sentimentality in which God's saving act in Christ is gratuitous

145

to the point of contingency. Tillich is therefore prepared to work with the concept of divine justice, not in the traditional penal sense, but as 'the act through which [God] lets the self-destructive consequences of existential estrangement go their way.'[34] He cannot remove them because they belong to the structure of being itself. The 'divine removal of guilt and punishment is not an act of overlooking the reality and depth of existential estrangement'. On the contrary: 'God's atoning activity must be understood as his participation in existential estrangement and its self-destructive consequences. He cannot remove these consequences; they are implied in his justice. But he can take them upon himself by participating in them and transforming them for those who participate in his participation.'[35] Tillich claims convincingly that this language, though profoundly symbolic, is also profoundly biblical. The Bible represents God as being patient, angry, compassionate, as changing his mind and as not sparing his Son, all of which expressions show what Tillich calls 'a freedom for concreteness in speaking of God's living reactions to the world of which theology is naturally afraid'.[36] In 'the Cross of the Christ the divine participation in existential estrangement becomes manifest'.[37] Tillich draws attention to his choice of the word 'manifest'. 'Manifestations are effective expressions not only communications. Something happens through a manifestation which has effects and consequences.'[38] This is the context in which Tillich sees the language of sacrifice and liturgy as having its proper reference. By participating 'in the New Being, which is the being of Jesus as the Christ, men also participate in the manifestation of the atoning act of God'.[39]

Tillich's guidelines are of course rooted in his existentialist philosophy; and philosophical fashions change. Nevertheless, I believe that he here puts forward a model with considerable possibilities for a relevant contemporary soteriology, even where one does not share, or at least totally share, his analysis of existence and transcendence. His basic model is estrangement, which he admittedly interprets in an existentialist sense but which is open to other kinds of interpretation, especially if we employ the synonym 'alienation', which has several points of resonance with contemporary cultures and preoccupations. Modern secular man will accept the concept of alienation where he would reject the term 'sin'. It is therefore appropriate for the Christian theologian to work out a soteriology based on the notion of reconciliation. In this task all the great patristic themes can be convincingly restated. Relevant preaching should not be the exclusive prerogative of Zulus.

NOTES

1. Cited in F. W. Dillistone, *The Christian Understanding of Atonement* (Welwyn, 1968). p. 112.
2. Ibid.
3. J. V. Taylor, *The Go-Between God: the Holy Spirit and The Christian Mission* (London, 1972), p. 50.
4. Irenaeus, *Adversus Haereses*, V, xvi, 3.
5. H. Rashdall, *The Idea of Atonement in Christian Theology* (London, 1919), p. 236.
6. Rashdall, op. cit., p. 237.
7. J. Riviere, *The Doctrine of the Atonement: A Historical Essay* (2 vols, London, 1909), vol. 1, p. 142.
8. G. Aulèn, *Christus Victor: An Historical Study of the Three Main Types of the Idea of the Atonement* (S.P.C.K. paperback edition, London, 1970), p. 17.
9. B. Altaner, *Patrology* (New York, 1960), p. 150.
10. F. L. Cross, *The Early Christian Fathers* (London, 1960), p. 110.
11. Rashdall, op. cit., p. 236.
12. Irenaeus, *Adversus Haereses* [*A.H.*], IV, xiv, 1.
13. *A.H.*, IV, xxxviii, 1.
14. *A.H.*, IV, xiv, 2.
15. *A.H.*, III, xxiii, 6.
16. *A.H.*, III, xx, 2.
17. *A.H.*, III, xxii, 3.
18. *A.H.*, III, xviii, 7.
19. *A.H.*, IV, xxxviii, 2.
20. Origen, *Comm. in Mattheum*, XVI, 8.
21. Gregory of Nyssa, *Oratio Catechetica*, 24.
22. S. Lyonnet and L. Sabourin, *Sin, Redemption, and Sacrifice: A Biblical and Patristic Study* (Rome, 1970), p. 203.
23. Tertullian, *De Pudicitia*, 2.
24. Tertullian, *De Poenitentia*, 5.
25. Jaroslav Pelikan remarks in his foreword to the 1970 edition: 'It is the criterion of a great work of theology that it sets the ground rules for a discussion even if that discussion goes beyond the original argument. Measured by this criterion, *Christus Victor* looks better all the time.' (p. xviii).
26. Aulèn, op. cit., p. 59.
27. R. W. Southern, *The Making of the Middle Ages* (London, 1953), pp. 219-257.
28. H. Gardner, 'The Dream of the Rood: An Exercise in Verse-translation', in W. W. Robson (ed.), *Essays and Poems Presented to Lord David Cecil* (London, 1970), p. 18.
29. Op. cit., p. 20.
30. R. W. Southern, *St Anselm and His Biographer: A Study of Monastic Life and Thought, 1059-c.1130* (Cambridge, 1966), p. 94. For discussion of the varying assessments of Anselm's soteriology see J.

McIntyre, *St Anselm and His Critics: A Re-interpretation of the Cur Deus Homo* (Edinburgh, 1954).
31. *Cur Deus Homo*, I, 20.
32. Southern, *St Anselm and his Biographer*, p. 113.
33. P. Tillich, *Systematic Theology* (Nisbet edit., Welwyn, 1968) Part III, pp. 196-208.
34. Tillich, loc. cit., p. 201.
35. Ibid.
36. Tillich, loc. cit., p. 202.
37. Ibid.
38. Ibid.
39. Tillich, loc. cit., p. 203.

CONTEMPORARY PERSPECTIVES
ON REDEMPTION THEOLOGY

Gabriel Daly, O.S.A.

'The very absence of explicit dogmatic and extensive polemical treatment of the meaning of salvation makes it necessary as well as hazardous to find some other scheme for organising the doctrinal material on this subject.'[1] Professor Pelikan's observation draws attention to an interesting problem in theological methodology. The doctrine of redemption, unlike the doctrine of the person of Christ, did not develop dialectically through positions and counter-positions until a synthesis was reached which could be imposed as orthodox on the Church by a council. Soteriology thus faces problems of a different character from those of christology. Significantly, we speak of christological *dogmas* but of *theories* of redemption.

It is perhaps initially tempting to regard the theology of redemption as a series of interpretations placed upon a given and uninterpreted fact. This temptation quickly withers in the light of even the most rudimentary awareness of the hermeneutical problem. Only a positivist can avoid the inescapable ambiguity built into the word history. Facts and events become 'historical' only after they have been selected, designated significant, and related to other facts and events similarly treated. The designation of events as 'saving' underlines still further the problems which arise out of a faith which is historically based. There are elements in Christian soteriology which would cause few problems to gnostics. The *Christus Victor* theme, for example, has something in common with gnostic dualism but is brought into conformity with Christian orthodoxy by an important modification of the dualism: The Devil, though a finite being, is allowed extensive influence over man, an influence out of all proportion to his intrinsic status. The result is a cosmic struggle between good and evil which reaches its culmination in the life, death, and resurrection of Christ.

Gustaf Aulen in his distinguished, though by no means impartial, study of the atonement describes this patristic theme as the 'Classic'

149

one and throws it into sharp contrast with Anselm's theory of satis-faction.[2] Aulen, however, does not discuss the reliance of both theories on the assumption of a coherence and homogeneity between transcend-ent being and historical existence. This coherent and homogeneous relationship is not seriously affected by a demythologising in the one case, or by a recognition of anthropomorphism in the other. In both theories the historical objectivity of Calvary is univocally related to the transcendent objectivity of its interpretation by Christian faith; and the transcendent interpretation is construed as 'objective' in roughly the same sense as the historical event it interprets. Eschatology here is seen as history prolonged into infinity. To use scholastic terms, in these theories *fides quae* is all; *fides qua* is little more than a window onto the transcendent scene in which the spectacle owes nothing to the spectator, and audience-participation is virtually an irrelevance.

It was Peter Abelard who first attempted to redress the balance of the extreme transcendalism of both the 'Classic' and Anselmian theories. He saw that a transcendentalised history must be matched by an historicised transcendence. The believer must participate in, and not merely look out upon, the drama of redemption. Thus Abelard took up a neglected patristic theme, that of Christ the Illuminator,[3] and in a much-quoted passage of his commentary on Romans gave his inter-pretation of Christ's redemptive work. God's Son 'took upon him our nature and in it taught us by word and example and so endured unto death, and thus bound us closer to himself by love'. 'Therefore our redemption is that supreme love which is in us through Christ's passion ... so that we fulfil all things from love rather than from fear of [God].'[4] Bernard of Clairvaux was the first, though by no means the last, critic to accuse Abelard of Pelagianism.[5] On the other hand, the nineteenth century liberals adopted him with all the surprised enthusi-asm they reserved for the mavericks of the middle ages. 'At last,' wrote Rashdall, 'we have found a theory of the atonement which thoroughly appeals to reason and to conscience.'[6] Both responses are partial, if not indeed tendentious. Today we are perhaps in a better position to appreciate that Abelard was rejecting neither the doctrine of grace nor the notion of a transcendent drama. He was supplying a much-needed existential corrective to an exclusive concern with that drama as bear-ing upon, but extrinsic to, man. As Richard Weingart has put it, Abe-lard's concern was to interiorise both man's predicament and Christ's correcting of that predicament. Abelard's 'teaching on the atonement has been justly praised for its insight into the nature and cure of man's alienation from God'.[7] He took seriously the psychological and moral dimension of salvation, which is why he strikes an answering chord not

150

alone in the liberals, but in twentieth century theologians also.

Abelard's contribution to soteriology inevitably raises the problem of the relationship between 'objective' and 'subjective' interpretations of redemption. Although some theologians express a dissatisfaction with the classification 'objective/subjective',[8] the distinction is a legitimate attempt to identify and label a real problem that will not go away simply because one dislikes the potentially disjunctive character of the terminology traditionally employed to deal with it. The distinction should not be taken as labelling two mutually exclusive theories or groups of theories. Rather it depicts a dialectical relationship in which one perspective complements the other and corrects the imbalance which results from an exclusive concentration on either. To appreciate this we need to consider the effect upon theology of Kant's philosophical revolution.

It is usually impossible to indicate precisely the beginnings of any movement in the history of thought. There is, however, a strong case to be made for taking Immanuel Kant as the starting point of modern theology. Almost everyone in the nineteenth century, Paul Tillich wrote, accepted Kant's critique as a presupposition. 'You will not find a [Protestant] theologian who has not accepted it, or modified it, and attempted to save what could be saved of natural theology after Kant's tremendous attack on it. Even a man like Karl Barth who is so firmly rooted in the classical tradition, has fully accepted the Kantian criticism of natural theology.'[9] Barth himself, in a striking phrase, remarked that Kant had offered 'terms of peace' to theology. But Kant, by his recognition of the evil inherent in man, also infuriated those of his contemporaries who wanted to prolong the Enlightenment's optimistic view of man's natural innocence. Thus, for example, Goethe wrote to Herder that Kant 'had criminally smeared his philosopher's cloak with the shameful stain of radical evil ... so that Christians too might yet be enticed to kiss its hem'.[10] Barth saw the significance of this reaction and expressed it in a graceful analogy. 'In Kant's philosophy, as in the music of Mozart, there is something of the calm and majesty of death which seems suddenly to loom up from afar to oppose the eighteenth-century spirit'.[11]

The eighteenth century had rejected with particular vehemence the doctrine of original sin. Kant in effect brought it back but offered man no remedy for it. Kantian man is saddled with the stern, indeed implacable, demands of duty. He has no need of, or possibility of receiving, redemption or grace. Moral experience is the only road to God — and it is an unredeemed moral experience. Kant leaves man alone with the stern demands of the categorical imperative but offers him no help in meeting those demands or forgiveness when he fails to meet them. Clearly, Christian thinkers who accepted Kant's critique of metaphysics and the implications of that critique for theology, had to ponder carefully where they now stood in respect of soteriology. There would be no place for devils and cosmic battles, or for any other happening outside the mind and heart of man. There would be no place either for Anselm's theory of satisfaction or for Luther's theory of penal substitution. Instead it would be taken for granted that all theology begins from a study of human dispositions, since only man's subjective religious response can be the object of scientific, critically aware, study. Experience, critically analysed, was to be the key to understanding religion. The liberals differed among themselves on whether that experience was moral or mystical.

Friedrich Schleiermacher accepted without question Kant's doctrine of immanence, but he reacted sharply against Kant's moralism. For Schleiermacher, 'Christian doctrines are accounts of the Christian religious affections set forth in speech'.[12] The attributes we ascribe to God 'are to be taken as denoting not something special in God, but only something special in the manner in which the feeling of absolute dependence is to be related to him'.[13] Salvation for Schleiermacher is the movement from self-consciousness to God-consciousness. He prefers to speak of 'consciousness of sin' rather than of sin as such. Consciousness of sin occurs whenever God-consciousness supervenes in our lives and turns self-consciousness into pain.[14] Schleiermacher maintains that 'the consciousness of sin never exists in the soul of the Christian without the consciousness of the power of redemption'.[15] This redemption comes from Christ. 'The Redeemer,' he says, 'assures believers into the power of His God-consciousness, and this is His redemptive activity'.[16] He communicates this God-consciousness to the community of his followers. Schleiermacher refuses to separate the passion and death of Jesus from the rest of his life. Jesus maintained the highest possible form of God-consciousness throughout his life. Every refusal of his contemporaries to share with him his God-consciousness was for him a deep suffering. His passion was the final intensification of this suffering.

The case against liberal theology put by Karl Barth and his contemporaries needs no restatement. The liberals, according to Barth, had reduced theology to anthropology. Man, not God, had become the focal point of their theological thought. Barth's 'theology of crisis' was a necessary moment in the continuing dialectic of theological reflection. But Barth can be properly appreciated only in the dialectical context of liberal theology. Instinctively conservative thinkers, both Evangelical and Catholic, can possess Barth too easily. Barth comes as a cheap grace to any theologian who has not passed in some way through the liberal experience and retained what is of permanent value in the liberal position. Conservative Roman Catholic theology is perhaps especially susceptible in this respect. To move from scholastic orthodoxy into Barthian, or any other kind of, neo-orthodoxy is to miss out an indispensable middle stage. The nineteenth century is by common consent one of the most important centuries in the history of theology; but Catholic theology went to ground during it, thus avoiding, and thereby merely postponing, a necessary phase in the normal historical evolution of religious thought. Catholic theology needs to recapituate (in the Irenaean sense) the nineteenth century experience before it is in a position to transcend and, where necessary, correct that experience. And not alone to transcend, but also to retain what was of value in liberal thought.

When Pius X's encyclical *Pascendi* (1907) lumped together most of the progressive Catholic thinkers of the age and labelled them 'immanentist', it condemned Catholic theology to sixty years of protective custody. The answer to exaggerated immanentism is, as Lucien Laberthonniere showed, a balanced theology of immanence, not a further and unnuanced emphasis on transcendent reality which is then superimposed on historical reality as if there were uninterrupted continuity and homogenity between them.[17]

Transcendent reality has to be refracted into symbol in order to become intelligible to man in history. No Christian doctrine demonstrates this symbolic refraction more clearly than that of the work of Christ. We form an impression of what it means to be saved in the eschatological sense from our immanent experience of the lesser salvations which occur in our individual and, more importantly, in our social lives.

The early middle ages found in the cosmic drama theory of redemption a strikingly relevant cultural expression of the doctrine of redemption. If our age is to find an expression of comparable relevance, it will have to look closely and sensitively at the forces, movements, and influences which contemporary man experiences as enslaving. It will then have to seek out and ponder the counter-forces which are experienced as liberating from that enslavement and draw from them its symbols of eschatological redemption, remembering always that the true symbol participates in the reality it refracts.[18] When we go about this search, we shall find that the New Testament models for expressing Christ's work have a timeless character about them, as long as we are prepared to give them fresh cultural relevance.

Before suggesting some directions such a search might take, I want to consider some objections which can be brought against the traditional presentation of the doctrine of redemption.

For centuries the presentation assumed the literal historicity of the biblical account of the creation and fall. The doctrine was deployed on a time-scale. Salvation had a history, and indeed a geography, in so far as the events interpreted as salvific took place in the ancient Near East. Down to and including its culmination on Golgotha it intersected with, and overlapped, a small segment of secular history. It raised the footnotes of that history to the status of chapter headings. A bunch of slaves escaping from Rameses II became a nation rescued by God, and their escape became an epic event celebrated in their own racial memory and literary monuments, and it was sacramentalised in a carefully-regulated cultic ceremony. The existence of this historical background enabled the first preachers of Christianity to interpret the death of their founder as the culminating event in that history. The death and resurrection of Jesus of Nazareth inaugurates the end-time and makes possible a break with the Torah.

Several problems arise out of this historicising of the saving process. As Christians we profess the death and resurrection of Jesus to be the decisive turning-point in human history. More than that, we proclaim that Jesus brings history to an end by his inauguration of a new age. Yet empirical history has carried on in many respects as if nothing radically salvific had happened; and for two thousand years the followers of Jesus have lived in that history, many of them also as if nothing salvific had happened. We are committed to the conviction that we live in the end-time. We look to a second coming as vindication of that conviction. Thus, psychologically at least, we are back in a period of expectation not dissimilar from that of the Jews. Alfred Loisy was stating an evident truth when he wrote that Jesus proclaimed the kingdom, and it was the Church which came.[19]

We proclaim that Church as the community of salvation, possibly hoping that our hearers do not know too much history or at least have piously selective memories. The history of the Church as institution is on balance more likely to disedify than edify. No amount of bluster about the spotless Bride of Christ can alter the secular squalor of large tracts of ecclesiastical history. Can we simply shrug off Nietzche's jibe that we shall have to look more saved before we can expect him to believe in our Saviour? Whatever theories of redemption we resort to as expressions of our faith, we are operating across a very large credibility gap. We need to have either great faith or great neck to appear on the streets of Belfast or Beirut crying 'Alleluia, we are a saved people living in the end-time when evil has been defeated and the reign of God has begun.' It is of course possible to meet these objections; but a little modest circumstantial embarrassment would become us while doing so.

Far more damaging to an effective soteriology is the traditional link between the doctrine of redemption and the doctrine of original sin understood as a great primal moral catastrophe occurring at the dawn of history and radically altering the subsequent course of that history. The First Adam/Second Adam parallel takes on a radically different frame of reference when Adam is interpreted as being the whole human race. The doctrine of original sin is in serious need of reinterpreation. Yet Protestant theologians tend to regard it as peripheral, while Catholics are apparently still hamstrung by their inability to find a hermeneutic of Church teaching which allows for scientific and critical changes of perspective. If creation is evolutionary, as scientific consensus indicates, then this fact has far-reaching implications for any credible theology of salvation. To ignore these implications is to damage the credibility of theology. The notion of sin is caught up in the evolutionary process, and this is, or ought to be, forcing us to take seriously what we always theoretically said we believed, namely, the sin is a mystery. It is part of the wider problem and mystery of evil, which is itself apparently inseparable from cosmic creation and historical existence. Nature is red in tooth and claw—and man belongs to nature. Therefore *in some way* redemption has an evolutionary character. This involves us in the difficult task of establishing a convincing relationship between evolutionary historical existence and eschatology. Only Teilhard and the Process theologians appear to have taken this problem with the seriousness it merits. One reason for hesitation in taking the question further would seem to be that it involves us in exploring the implications of the hitherto unthinkable notion that God is creating a world with 'evil' and 'sin' as inevitable elements in it. The doctrine of redemption reflected this unwillingness to ascribe the existence of 'evil' and 'sin' to God by postulating a redemptive process only *after* man had subverted God's original plan. Thus it had to appeal to an idyllic original state where nature was *not* red in tooth and claw and where the lion lay down with the lamb. Contemporary science does not allow us to postulate such a primal state; and we have yet to accept the far-reaching theological implications of this.

These objections need to be carefully pondered when we seek to construct a contemporary theology of sin and redemption.

Theories of redemption necessarily reflect (1) our idea of God, (2) our idea of the Church, and (3) our idea of sin.

1. *Our Idea of God*

Since our idea of God is necessarily formed from the projection onto an infinite screen of a congeries of human characteristics and needs, we must constantly remind ourselves that no human conception of God is ever free of material for idolatry, and that many conceptions of God have in fact been projections onto God of some of man's meanest and most ignoble facets. Much traditional soteriology, Catholic and Protestant, was designed to complement a notion of God an an inflexible legislater, judge, and punisher. Now while there is a sense in which each of these divine functions can be healthily understood, there is also a sense in which they can be made to satisfy our own neurotic needs. Thus if God the punisher is a postulate of man's neurotic need to be punished, it follows that a recognition of the neurosis for what it is, that is, a pathological condition in need of healing, will involve a correspondingly purified image of the sovereignty of God. True, neurosis can sometimes stimulate a highly significant and valuable theology, as can be seen for instance in the case of Kierkegaard. (Kierkegaard, however, is almost unique among theologians in that *he knew* he was neurotic.) Man's first redemptive need is to be freed of his unnamed fears and of the morally and religiously crippling anxieties and pessimisms which afflect his relationship both with God and with his fellow men and women.

An unwavering and incessantly realised conviction of

'. . . the absolute paternal care
That will not leave us, but prevents us everywhere.'[20]

is the irreplaceable foundation of an attitude and behaviour which reflects not so much the mere idea as the lived experience of being saved. Forgiving is a costly business—for God as well as for man. There is a magnificent, though implicit, soteriology in Dag Hammarskjöld's penetrating insight into forgiveness.

Forgiveness breaks the chain of causality because he who 'forgives' you—out of love—takes upon himself the consequences of what *you* have done. Forgiveness, therefore, always entails a sacrifice.

The price you must pay for your own liberation through another's sacrifice, is that you in turn must be willing to liberate in the same way, irrespective of the consequences to yourself.[21]

Perhaps we human beings overrate our natural capacity for giving and receiving forgiveness and thus fail to realise how difficult it is for us to entertain, and rest in, the idea of a truly forgiving God. Forgiveness as

156

an abstraction we can handle. The reality is another matter. The history of canonical practice in the Church suggest that we cannot bear too much forgiving.

2. Our Idea of the Church

Healing and reconciliation, that is, redemptive grace, come to us sacramentalised by the community's willingness to receive, to understand, to forgive, and to encourage. The healing community is a normal vehicle of divine reconciliation, and it provides all the deepest symbols for appreciating and accepting the divine acceptance. The healing community enables us to make divine forgiveness an experienced reality in our lives by enabling and encouraging us to forgive ourselves as well as others. In his book *The Atonement*, the late Bishop F. R. Barry wrote: 'Any defensible doctrine of Atonement would seem to require both a high Christology and a high theology of the Church.' He continued: 'But the Church is that part of the total world in which [Christ] is recognised as Lord and Saviour, and it is the unique instrument of redemption—unique with the uniqueness of Christ himself.'[22] Bishop Barry's point is theologically indisputable and should prompt us to wonder why ready acceptance and forgiveness have not always been among the most prominent characteristics of the intitutional Church down the ages.

3. Our Idea of Sin

All of which is of course closely bound up with the third matter which reflects, and is reflected into, one's theories of redemption, namely, one's idea of sin. Here I want to concentrate on just one element in a very wide topic. We speak of the *mystery* of sin but often end up treating it, in practice, as nothing other than ethical failure. Admittedly the grosser kinds of quantification and calculation are no longer practised, but the sweet reasonableness and tolerance which grace the pages of moral theology today, however welcome a change they may be from the rigidity and legalism of the past, seem to be uncomfortable with a dimension of sin which, for want of an agreed and satisfactory term, one can only call 'mysterious' or even 'mystical'. Some years ago *The Times Literary Supplement* carried a review of one of Bernard Haring's books. 'Dr Haring,' said the reviewer, 'underestimates the intense attractiveness and force of the demonic: he seems to be the voice of a reforming church, not of a secular age beset with devils.'[23] That remark seems to me to raise a fascinating point which has an obvious relevance to soteriology. In our reforming search for the roots of morality may we not be overlooking the dimension of mystery and even of perverted

157

mysticism which can attach to some manifestations of evil? Today's resurgence of interest in magic, demonism, gothic films, and in general in the occult, might be interpreted as a popular rediscovery of the daimonic forces in man which have been denied by secular rationalism, but facile social and political optimism, and even by Christian moralists seeking to escape from the rigidities and insensitivities of the past.

A purely sociological explanation of evil is one of the most unsatisfactory kinds of moral reductionism. Liberal sociology, as a wit has put it, seems to regard goats as sheep from deprived backgrounds. Of course broken homes, economic deprivation, or a childhood starved of affection are all seed-beds of delinquency. What we should avoid, however, is the reduction of delinquency and crime, without remainder, either to the mere misues of freedom or to circumstantial deprivation. That deprivation merely serves to release and stimulate forces which the delinquent may not recognise as existing within himself, much less see the need to harness and control. In a world of apathy and alienation the expression of violence, hatred and aggression is a way of communicating, not just with others but even with oneself. For such people a perverted experience is preferable to no experience at all. Delinquency of this kind is surely much more than revenge upon society or a cry for help. It may be either or both of these, but it is also a handing over of the self to its own daimonic forces.

The contest between Augustine and the Pelagians left the Western Church with a strong but perplexing conviction, as initially disturbing as it is ultimately hopeful: to be human is to be in need of redemption. Human 'sinfulness' precedes exposure to a sinful situation or environment. It is in tackling this problem that existentially-based theologies are often at their weakest. 'Sin' precedes *Dasein*—a thought which might encourage us to take more seriously the analogical meaning of 'sin' as an index to the tragic dimension of being human. No worthwhile theology of sin can afford to ignore Ivan Karamazov's searing and compassionate cry of rebellion or to speak lightly about 'the tears with which the earth is saturated from its crust to its centre'. By no means all of those tears are the result of personal or social sin. One can moralise too soon, too often, and too compulsively. Instead of attending in some awe to the grey area where culpability shades off into tragedy until it is finally swallowed up in the mystery of life itself, we persist in asking who was to blame, this man or his parents? Jesus's answer to that question recalls Yahweh's withering judgement on the shallow moralising of Job's friends: 'Who is this that darkens counsel by words without knowledge?' (Job 38:2). To adopt culpability as a controlling concept in the theology of original sin is, if not to darken

158

counsel, at least to cripple the possibilities of that theology from the outset.[24]

Soteriology presents us with problems today precisely because many of the ingredients of the traditional understanding of redemption are no longer either credible or tolerable. What happens to the traditional teaching on redemption when one no longer accepts the literal truth of an initial paradise, a primal moral catastrophe which introduced sin, alienation, and pain into the world, and an angry God who demands a satisfaction achieved by the atrocious suffering of his own Son? Calvary does not *explain* the mystery of suffering and the role it plays in the divine plan. On the contrary, the burden of that mystery is aggravated by the spectacle of a crucified God. We believe and affirm that there is a profound and awe-inspring truth in all this; but how do we detach this truth from the myths traditionally employed to express it, myths which our dull imaginations have allowed to collapse into flat literalism and which have consequently lost their power to speak to us authentically? And what do we do with the concept of sacrifice when we have rejected the notion of an angry God being propitiated or of an oriental despot receiving the abject obeisances of his subject and have come to the recognition that true adoration enhances the worth and dignity of the adorer. The problem is not restricted to systematic theology. The Letter to the Hebrews is a difficult text to interpret today once we leave the *hortus conclusus* of academic criticism and face the challenge of relevant preaching. Harnack observed nearly eighty years ago that the language of sacrifice and propitiation was necessary if Christian belief and worship were to penetrate the culture and consciousness of the first century.[25] But that culture and that consciousness have changed radically—a point which has been made painfully clear by recent attempts at a newly authenticated theology of priesthood.

The alleged crisis of identity in the priesthood today is often explained sociologically in terms of role. This attempt to give a sociological explanation of the crisis is at best only a partial one, and at worst is a distraction from deeper theological analysis. It is not simply the *role* of the priest, but the very *concept of priesthood*, which presents interpretative problems today. Of the three traditional roles ascribed to Christ, priest, prophet, and king, only that of prophet, I would suggest, has an *immediate* relevance in contemporary Western culture. In an age of protest, social criticism, and struggles for political freedom one can expect the prophetic role of Christ to be emphasised, while his kingship and priesthood are less easy to interpret to a world increasingly uncomfortable with the overtones of autocracy associated with both. Thus there was an almost disproportionate symbolic resonance in the *priest*, Camilo Torres, leaving his ecclesiastical flock behind and taking to revolutionary existence in the hills of Colombia.

Contemporary soteriology reflects, as one would expect it to do, the problems, hesitations and diffidence which are evident in all responsible theology today. In particular it reflects the problems which arise out of attempts to conceptualise and speak authentically about God and about Christ as God-man. Furthermore, as I have suggested, it is profoundly affected by increasing emphasis on the Church as a saving community in and for the world, and by a theology of sin which is striving to get beyond mere moralising by taking in the mystery of existence itself. In this respect, however, the work done by German theologians from Barth onwards remains surprisingly unadventurous. Thus, for example, Pannenberg arranges his soteriology around the concept of substitution, while Kasper's recent book on christology is more concerned with the person than with the work of Christ. Moltmann is perhaps the theologian most obviously concerned with soteriology today. Both he and J. B. Metz appear to be redressing the balance of a theology that had become too preoccupied with the future. In a lecture, 'Redemption and Emancipation' (1973) Metz mentions the need for a 'solidarity backwards'. (He attaches considerable importance to Christ's descent among the dead.) He speaks of the need to avoid 'second-order Darwinism as objective cynicism in which the sorrows of the past, as Ivan Karamazov bitterly put it, serve only as manure for future harmony'. Metz concludes: 'No purely systematic theology is capable of providing an honest theological "mediation" between redemption and the meaning of suffering'. Perhaps we have here a pointer to the development of soteriology. The traditional Christian understanding of suffering has not always had great theological depth. The mystics *practised* the truth and had an intuitive grasp of its meaning, while the theologians, preoccupied with justice, judgement and punishment, failed signally to relate the mystery of suffering to the mystery of existence. Suffering was for them merely an externally-imposed punishment which was partly retributive and partly corrective. The case against this punitive conception of suffering rests on two contemporary convictions. First, it seriously misrepresents the nature of God; and, second, it notably fails to recognise that the natural and historical structure of creation, on this planet at least, is utterly inseparable from the phenomenon of pain. The beauty of the gazelle and the grace of its movement are the product of its need to escape the jaws of its predators. Pain is written into the very primal laws of life; and the man or woman who is not initially scandalised by this runs the risk of trivialising the theology of redemption.

Any worthwhile theology of redemption has to attempt to find and affirm meaning in the tears of things. Contemporary *theologia crucis* is opening out to this dimension of saving history. 'As soon as you say incarnation,' writes Hans Urs von Balthasar, 'you say cross.' Moltmann, who quotes this remark of Balthasar, gives a trinitarian context to the theology of the cross.[26] He goes so far as to say that trinitarian theology derives its meaning from the cross of Christ—a remark which would have shocked many of the Church Fathers and would have seemed utterly incomprehensible to the scholastics. Moltman, however, takes pain and death with all the seriousness and existential awareness of secular man. He refuses to make acceptance of them a cheap grace. Calvary shows us the involvement of God in the human predicament.

> The crucified Christ must be thought of as the *origin of creation* and the embodiment of the eschatology of being. In the cross of his Son, God took upon himself not only death, so that man might be able to die comforted with the certainty that even death could not separate him from God, but still more, in order to make the crucified Christ the ground of his new creation, in which death itself is swallowed up in the victory of life and there will be 'no sorrow, no crying, and no more tears'.[27]

Moltmann's words have a deceptively familiar ring. They sound Alexandrian, but without the suggestion of a defective humanity. They appear to by-pass the Chalcedonian formula of one person in two natures; but they do not contradict it. They reflect adversely not on what Chalcedon set out to teach but on the use to which later christology put that teaching. The doctrine of the two natures became necessary only after the Alexandrian theologians had impaired, or appeared to impair, a proper recognition of Christ's full manhood. The Antiochene rejection of Cyril's *mia physis* was in some respects a tragic consequence of an over-speculative theological debate. All the contestants agreed that we are not permitted to say that the Father suffered and died. But the problem extended further than that: Christian hellenism recoiled from saying that 'God suffered and died'. Two far-reaching and highly sophisticated qualifications were necessary before the Greek mind could be brought to face the philosophical scandal of a crucified God: The Son of God, distinct in person from the Father, suffered and died in a human nature distinct from the divine nature of his person.

Contemporary dogmatic theologians may be forgiven a furtive sigh and a perhaps repressed yearning to return to the marvellous simplicity of the Pauline 'God was in Christ reconciling the world to himself'.

How many preachers and teachers, impeccably orthodox in their trinitarian formulae, are tritheists in spite of their intentions? (The conservative call to catechists to put more 'doctrine' into their programmes occasionally strikes one as the product of a deficiency in knowledge of the character and history of Church doctrine.)

By way of conclusion I should like to focus what I have been saying into some theses for consideration.

1. We may fruitfully speak of the objective and subjective dimensions of redemption, if we understand the objectivity in question to be, not historical, but transcendent. History is inescapably and radically immanent. Christ's victory over sin and death is transcendentally objective and as such is open, not to historical, but only to eschatological verification. Faith is the interpretative process, involving heart as well as mind, which enables us to affirm that the political failure of the historical life and death of Jesus of Nazareth was in reality the greatest triumph in human history with transcendent meaning for mankind, past, present and to come.

2. Transcendent values, however, though objectively and eminently real, are mediated to man through his immanent experience of the symbols which are written into his cultural existence. These symbols *contain*, and not merely represent, the reality they symbolise. Gregory Baum in his recent book *Religion and Alienation* makes a plea, reminiscent of Coleridge's, for cultivating the imagination as *the* religious faculty. 'If divine revelation takes place in symbols, then the imagination is its proper locus in the human mind.'[28] The cross has proved to be a symbol of illimitable possibilities. The sign of contradiction becomes the fullest affirmation of meaning and hope. This paradox lies at the very heart of graced existence; but it is intuition and imagination, rather than discursive reason, which respond most compellingly to its symbolic expression.

3. Our symbols must be taken from lived reality experienced from the inside, if not directly, at least by imaginative participation. Literature, art, and music all have an important role in intensifying experiences already present, though perhaps not more than seminally so, at first hand. Examples from literature and the figurative arts abound and need no comment or recommendation. The possibilities of music, for those sensitive to its power, are also evident enough. Gustav Mahler's view that 'music should always express yearning, a yearning beyond the things of this world',[29] expresses an essentially romantic aesthetic, but it reminds us that even, and perhaps especially, in our anti-romantic age, the yearning celebrated by the nineteenth century romantics

retains its relevance as a vehicle of religious experience. Music, however, offers other symbolic possibilities. Webern's orchestration of the *Ricercare* from Bach's *Musical Offering* can be seen as an aural myth of two worlds in conflict. Bach's endlessly ebbing and flowing music expresses unity through a succession of interwoven lines all coalescing into a massive and unified structure. Webern by his fragmented orchestration takes this unified structure asunder and reassembles it strand by strand, giving us a divided world with all the restless fragmentation of our age; yet, because it leaves Bach's notes unchanged, Webern's diffused wisps of sound speak of a harmony and unity mysteriously lost to us but somehow endowed with the radiant hope of being regained.

4. Of all the traditional symbolic models for expressing the mystery of sin and redemption, perhaps alienation and reconciliation speak most tellingly to our age. Alienation is a term with both political and psychological resonances. Liberation theology is striving to realise the possibilities of sacramentalising the struggle for freedom, justice, and the dignity of man. The positive qualities of this theology are already widely acknowledged; but the specific potential it holds out for revitalising soteriology is not without its drawbacks. If the remedy for political and economic alienation is found in violent revolution, the theological language employed to reflect it will be one which speaks of sacrifice, blood, purification, and readiness to suffer and inflict wounds and death for the sake of victory. The danger of sacramentalising a military process lies in the attempt it may make to give a mystical significance to the *act* of revolution, thus construing redemption as a never-ending series of revolutions (unless one believes in the possibility of secular Utopias).

Non-violent revolution avoids the danger of this kind of false mysticism, and the proponents of non-violent revolution are unquestionably among the leading prophets of today. They can speak of sacrifices, victims, and victory in a more convincingly Christian way because they do not have the daunting task of showing how you can shoot a man with love in your heart. They are also more ready to speak of reconciliation and less likely to make a permanent virtue of the *act* of revolution. They freely and courageously accept the implications of being political victims rather than would-be military victors. Their victory therefore has something of the moral grandeur of Christ's cross.

5. All revolutionaries, however, might profitably ponder a sober truth stated not long ago by E. R. Norman in a lecture entitled 'The Political Implications of the Doctrine of Original Sin'.

> When a man takes up good or moral political causes, his inherent level of sin flows into them as much as into anything else. A man

who adopts a morally corrupt position over one issue may also adopt many other positions which are morally unexceptionable; and, conversely, those who clamour for social righteousness over one selected issue may be soaked in immoral attitudes in all other parts of their personalities. Because that is so, political action is often a poor instrument to put the world's sins to rights.[30]

So far from being a plea for political inaction, these words express an important contemporary restatement of a basic Augustinian insight. 'Because Christian pessimism is realistic,' says Dr Norman, 'it is full of real compassion about *all* the opinions and behaviour of men. It supplies the proper motive for Christian involvement with human suffering.'

6. Alienation is a term with powerful psychological resonances. Erich Neumann has written that the essential fate of contemporary man is enacted on three fronts: the external world of extrahuman events, the community as the sphere of interhuman relationships, and the psyche as the world of interior human experience.[31] Neumann's point is that these three areas were once a unity, but evolutionary progress has separated each from the others while at the same time intensifying them. In a word, continuing hominisation produces an inevitable alienation in each of Neumann's three spheres. To read the early chapters of Genesis in the light of this insight is to release a flood of light on some of the most powerful pages in the Bible. It enables us to realise that creation is still going on. Man is still being formed from the slime of the earth. He continues to delight in the earth from which he has been taken, but his delight is marred by his inevitable alienation from his environment. Through eating of the tree of knowledge he continues to lose a lower and simpler harmony while acquiring a higher and more complex destiny. He must fall in order to rise; he must forfeit the peace and harmony appropriate to a lower form of existence in order to face the challenge of a higher form. He has no choice in the matter. (This, one notes in passing, is how Paul Tillich interprets the divine justice.[32]) Man is expelled from the paradise of an unintelligent and unfree peace and is consigned to the agony of intelligence and freedom. He must subdue the earth, but he is learning that the earth will tolerate only certain kinds of subjugation. He must live with his brothers, who by their very existence challenge his subjectivity, as Abel challenged Cain's. Finally he has to learn how to live with himself. Condemned to the rigours of freedom, he will constantly be tempted to lay down his burden and seek the security of unfreedom.[33]

7. At this point we are ripe for the central insights of the great Christian existentialists. Man, as they see him, must answer God's painful call to authenticity. He must have the courage to be. He must face the

justice of God as manifested in all the phenomena and experiences which bring about human alienation. He must come to an ever deepening realisation that simply to exist is to be in need of healing and atonement. In Eliot's marvellous words we are called to accept that

Our only health is the disease. . .
And that, to be restored, our sickness must grow worse.
The whole earth is our hospital. . . [34]

The surgeon who comes to heal us is, with mysterious simultaneity, from God and from our stock and is himself wounded. He alone has had the courage to be; he alone has faced all the implications of divine justice; he alone has experienced alienation to the very depths of his being and has met all its demands. He paid the price of being the perfect man, the totally human expression of God.

'If Jesus paid that price,' asks Dr David Stafford-Clark, 'whose was the bill? And why was it presented?'[35] And with that question, asked by a twentieth century psychiatrist, we are back in the world of the early Fathers. In different language, and from a different culture, they were asking the same question, a question which probes the mystery of life itself.

NOTES

1. J. Pelikan, *The Emergence of the Catholic Tradition (100-600)* (Chicago & London, 1971), p. 142. See F. W. Dillistone, *The Christian Understanding of Atonement* (Welwyn, 1968), for an interesting organisation of the material into models and analogues.
2. G. Aulèn, *Christus Victor: An Historical Study of the Three Main Types of the Idea of the Atonement* (SPCK, edit. London, 1970).
3. H. E. W. Turner, *The Patristic Doctrine of Redemption* (London, 1952), gives a four-fold classification of patristic theories of redemption: Christ the Illuminator, Christ the Victor, Christ the Deifier, and Christ the Victim.
4. P. Abelard, *Expositio in Epistolam ad Romanos*, III, iii, PL 178, 836.
5. St Bernard, *Letter 190*, analysed in A. Victor Murray, *Abelard and St Bernard: A Study in Twelfth Century "Modernism'* (Manchester, 1967) pp. 72-88.
6. H. Rashdall, *The Idea of Atonement in Christian Theology* (London, 1919), p. 360.
7. R. E. Weingart, *The Logic of Divine Love: A Critical Analysis of the Soteriology of Peter Abailard* (Oxford, 1970), p. 205.
8. See for example J. Macquarrie, *Principles of Christian Theology* (London, 1966), p. 286.
9. P. Tillich, *Perspectives on 19th Century and 20th Century Protestant Theology* (London, 1967), p. 64.

165

10. K. Barth, *Protestant Theology in the Nineteenth Century* (London, 1972), p. 294.
11. K. Barth, op. cit., p. 269.
12. F. Schleiermacher, *The Christian Faith,* English translation of the Second German edition, edited by H. R. Mackintosh and J. S. Stewart (Edinburgh, 1928), p. 76.
13. Schleiermacher, op. cit., p. 194.
14. Op. cit., p. 271.
15. Op. cit., p. 272, with note citing Romans 7:25; 8:2.
16. Op. cit., p. 425.
17. L. Laberthonnière, 'Le dogmatisme moral', first published in *Revue du Clergé Français,* vols 38 and 39 (1898). Reprinted in *Le réalisme chrétien: Précédé de Essais de philosophie religieuse* (Paris, 1966), pp. 39-108.
18. See P. Ricoeur, *The Symbolism of Evil* (New York, 1967), pp. 14-18.
19. A. Loisy, *L'Évangile et L'Église* (Paris, 1902), p. 111. It should perhaps be pointed out that Loisy intended no irony in this sometimes misunderstood remark.
20. T. S. Eliot, *Four Quartets* (Faber paperback edition, London, 1959), p. 30.
21. D. Hammarskjöld, *Markings,* translated by Leif Sjöberg and W. H. Auden (London, 1966), p. 163.
22. F. R. Barry, *The Atonement* (London, 1968), p. 183.
23. *Times Literary Supplement,* 26 July 1974.
24. This paragraph is reproduced from my review of P. Gulluy (ed.), *La culpabilité fondamentale: Péché originel et anthropologie moderne* (Lille, 1975) in *The Heythrop Journal* 18 (1977) 232-233.
25. A. Harnack, *What is Christianity?* (4th edition, London, 1923), p. 137.
26. J. Moltmann, *The Crucified God* (London, 1974), p. 205.
27. J. Moltmann, op. cit., p. 127, emphasis added.
28. G. Baum, *Religion and Alienation: A Theological Reading of Sociology* (New York, 1975), p. 244.
29. Cited in Henry-Louis de La Grange, *Mahler,* vol. 1 (London, 1974), p. 524.
30. I cite Dr Norman's words from a radio talk; the punctuation is thus speculative.
31. E. Neumann, *The Origin and History of Consciousness* (London, 1964), p. 267. I owe this reference to Dillistone, op. cit., p. 7. Dr Dillistone devotes a stimulating chapter to 'Alienation and Atonement'.
32. P. Tillich, *Systematic Theology,* vol. II (Nisbet edit., Welwyn, 1968), pp. 200-203.
33. St Augustine's analysis of the concept of peace in *De Civitate Dei,* XIX, 13, offers interesting possibilities, if read in this light.
34. T. S. Eliot, *Four Quartets,* pp. 29-30.
35. D. Stafford-Clark, *Five Questions in Search of an Answer* (Fontana Books, London, 1970), p. 94.